Why should business be ethical? What are the ethical standards which apply in a business context? How can business people set about making the ethical decisions which affect their practice and performance?

This book looks at business ethics from the perspective of the business practitioner, but with the rigour of the moral philosopher. Intended for introductory students of business, commerce and management studies, *Business ethics at work* begins by setting business clearly in the context of creating value for its owners, and develops a practical ethical decision model which can be simply and relevantly applied to the hard moral choices with which business people are faced day to day.

Against this background, some of the major ethical issues which arise in business are explored, for example, in human resource management, finance, marketing and advertising, the management of the environment and corporate governance. In conclusion, the book looks at the nature of ethical audit and argues that, for the business of the future, the identification of its ethical values and their integration into its policies and practices, will be a crucial ingredient of success.

ad hoc —

exclusively for some
understood purpose

BUSINESS ETHICS AT WORK

BUSINESS ETHICS
AT WORK

ELIZABETH VALLANCE

CAMBRIDGE
UNIVERSITY PRESS

PUBLISHED BY THE PRESS SYNDICATE OF THE UNIVERSITY OF CAMBRIDGE
The Pitt Building, Trumpington Street, Cambridge, United Kingdom

CAMBRIDGE UNIVERSITY PRESS
The Edinburgh Building, Cambridge CB2 2RU, UK
40 West 20th Street, New York, NY 10011–4211, USA
10 Stamford Road, Oakleigh, VIC 3166, Australia
Ruiz de Alarcón 13, 28014 Madrid, Spain
Dock House, The Waterfront, Cape Town 8001, South Africa

http://www.cambridge.org

First published 1995
Reprinted 1996, 1998, 2001

Printed in the United Kingdom at the University Press, Cambridge

A catalogue record for this book is available from the British Library

Library of Congress Cataloguing in Publication data
Vallance, Elizabeth (Elizabeth M.)
Business ethics at work/Elizabeth Vallance.
p.   cm.
Includes bibliographical references and index.
ISBN 0 521 40535 1. – ISBN 0 521 40568 8 (pbk.)
1. Business ethics.   2. Management–Moral and ethical aspects.
I. Title.
HF 5387.V34   1995
174'.4–dc20   94 32431   CIP

ISBN 0 521 40535 1 hardback
ISBN 0 521 40568 8 paperback

For Iain, Rachel and Edmund

Contents

Acknowledgements

I have bent the ears of so many people in the course of this book's rather long gestation that it seems invidious to mention some and not others. I am grateful to all the people in business and in Business Schools who have taken time to talk to me, generously to share ideas and to put me right on points of fact.

Much continuing inspiration has come from Professor Jack Mahoney, formerly of King's College, University of London and now of the London Business School, and Professor Charles Handy of the London Business School. Even when we have disagreed, I have found their ideas consistently challenging and relevant. Equally, I am grateful to my old friend and colleague, Dr Elaine Sternberg, for our many discussions.

Mike Lymath of HMV Group Ltd gave me much interesting background on human resource issues; Sir Adrian Cadbury educated me in corporate governance and Sir Jeremy Morse made me think about banking ethics. The faults that remain are, of course, mine. Richard Fisher, my editor at Cambridge University Press, has been that priceless combination of supportiveness and patience which authors crave but seldom get. Margaret Deith, also of Cambridge, helped me to focus some of my ideas, particularly in the early part of the book. I am grateful to them all.

This has not been an easy book to write: for a number of reasons, both professional and personal, it has been subject to stops and starts. Because of this, the most important debt I owe is to my family. My children, Rachel and Edmund, have kept me fed and made me laugh and my husband, Iain Vallance, has read most of the text as it came hot off the word processor and eliminated some of my lapses in logic in discussing many of the issues with his usual robustness and clarity. The book is for them, with my love and thanks.

PART I

The ethical framework

Introduction

There is something curiously bleak about the word 'ethics': it suggests a brake on natural exuberance, the substitution of what we ought for what we want and, above all, seems to threaten a largely academic discussion of moral philosophies. When used in relation to business it is particularly confusing as what ethical analysis can offer to business practice is not immediately apparent. Philosophers may be fascinated by the competing claims of deontological (i.e. rule-governed) theories and utilitarian (i.e. happiness-maximising) ones: this book is not for them. It is for the student of business rather than the student of philosophy, and for those who are trying to decide what to do for the best in the real world. It sets out to present a practical ethical framework which is clearly relevant to the moral dilemmas of business.

This scenario, however, assumes that business people will accept the general principle that an ethical framework of some kind has relevance for business. This is not necessarily the case, for there is often a feeling, among managers and others, that business is about making profits and ethics is about being good and, realistically, never the twain shall meet. Being a tough-minded manager implies that there's no time for the ethical niceties. There is sometimes also a deeper suspicion among managers that calls for value statements in business or the demand for more ethical business practices are really just a thinly disguised anti-capitalism or a generalised complaint against business and its aims and aspirations by those who disapprove of the profit motive or of market mechanisms.

Again, the currently fashionable talk about the 'social responsibility' of business has been seen by some managers as an attempt to force business to take on the role of government: to protect the environment; to regenerate the inner cities; to deal with everything that is wrong with society, from educational deprivation to racism.

3

I shall argue, however, that business ethics properly understood is neither anti-business nor anti-capitalist in its inspiration and operation. It is not a supercilious attempt to identify the pathologies of modern corporations and put them right with simplistic solutions; nor is it the instrument of devious government desires to offload its own social responsibilities onto business. Rather, it is a way of approaching business decisions systematically; seen in this way, it is quite simply a tool for helping managers to make choices that are often difficult. It involves articulating a coherent set of values for a business and trying to set decision-making within the context of these values. It is in this sense as fundamental to the running of the business as proper management accounts; without either, there is no direction and there are no controls; the business is running blind.

Business ethics is thus a branch of practical ethics. It is a relatively new area of study in this country and is consequently in the process of developing both a language in which its practitioners can communicate unequivocally and a theoretical framework within which business activity can be analysed and which will aid decision-taking. The tendency thus far has been to look to moral philosophy's classical theories – like Kantian deontology and Utilitarian rationalism, or their modern manifestations, to provide such frameworks. These theories are, however, concerned primarily with personal ethics; they do not address directly the kind of ethical problems that arise within a business context. Attempts to apply them to business have therefore not been entirely satisfactory. What I want to suggest here is at least the beginnings of a rather more focused framework, starting and emerging from the nature and aim of business itself.

A decision model for business ethics is undoubtedly a highly ambitious enterprise but if it begins to set some theoretical parameters, however imperfect at this stage, it will be worth while.

WHY ETHICS NOW?

It has been suggested recently that 'business ethics' is just a passing fashion a bit like muesli and jogging, which will come and go and can therefore be safely ignored or dismissed. Similar claims are made about, for example, corporate identity and total quality, which are regarded by some as little more than slick marketing moves by which companies sell themselves, internally and externally, as approachable, concerned and responsible. It is, however, no accident that businesses are increasingly searching for ways of relating to their staff and customers and, although my argument in this book is that there is a permanent and irreducible moral dimension to business decisions, there are historical reasons why interest in business ethics is particularly strong now.

Since at least the 1970s, questions about corporate governance, that is, the way in which business is organised and held responsible, have been raised. In the process, sometimes directly, sometimes indirectly, discussion has centred on the place of business in society. In the past, this was largely taken for granted: business existed to contribute to economic growth and the creation of higher living standards. But as growth itself ceased to be a superordinate goal and, indeed, has been challenged by some as a goal at all, so the aims and purposes of business have been increasingly debated. The Bullock Report, as long ago as 1977, raised the whole question of industrial democracy, of who ought to have power, from whom, to do what in organisations.[1] It proposed that employees should be represented on the boards of companies and, although this was rejected in many quarters as a negation of the principle that boards should be unitary rather than collections of representatives of different interests, it encouraged discussion of the role of employees, their rights and duties.

Slightly earlier, the Watkinson Report for the CBI marked a watershed in thinking about the role of business in society and, in effect, challenged both business leaders and legislators to rethink out-of-date legal and corporate structures.[2] Companies should be encouraged, the report said, to recognise duties and obligations not only to shareholders but to employees, customers, suppliers and society at large. This identification of the many constituencies of companies, of what have come to be called their stakeholders, was crucial to the later emphasis on social responsibility.

[1] Committee of Enquiry on Industrial Democracy (The Bullock Report) Cmnd. 6706, 1977.
[2] The Responsibilities of the British Public Company, CBI Company Affairs Committee (The Watkinson Report), CBI, 1973.

Across the Atlantic analysis of the social position of American companies was already well advanced. In a speech at Harvard Business School in 1969, Henry Ford II said: 'the terms of the contract between industry and society are changing ... Now we are being asked to serve a wider range of human values and to accept an obligation to members of the public with whom we have no commercial transactions.'[3]

At the same time, British business began to realise that it lagged behind much of Western Europe in its views of company obligations, especially to employees. The rights of employees, particularly to information about their company, had been emphasised by both Watkinson and Bullock and were progressively incorporated into legislation thereafter. It was later extended to include the general interests of employees.[4]

In addition, the enormous volume of recommendations, directives, codes of conduct, etc. which were beginning to emanate from the Commission of the European Community provided another set of parameters to be considered in the reassessment of company roles and responsibilities.[5] The impact of consumerism, environmentalism, feminism and anti-racism was increasingly felt by British business. Such concerns had begun as marginal interests pursued by what could comfortably be dismissed as lunatic fringes and which business could largely safely ignore. By the 1980s, however, organised consumer power was clearly here to stay, 'environmentally friendly' products were big business, and firms were competing to show that they were equal opportunities employers.

At the end of 1989, the European Commission adopted the action programme of the European Social Charter. Under this programme, the Commission is drawing up directives, which have the force of law in the member states, concerning, among other things, health and safety at work, contracts, local employment, and women's employment.[6] The Commission is keen to advance what is now being called the 'People's Europe' and

[3] Quoted in T. Donaldson, *Corporations and Morality*, Prentice-Hall, 1982, p. 36.
[4] See The Company Act, 1985, section 309.
[5] For a taste of the scope of EC involvement with business practice see e.g. *Operations of the European Community concerning Small and Medium-sized Enterprises*, Office of official publications of the EEC, 1988.
[6] See e.g. report in *Women of Europe*, no. 62, November–December 1989, p. 3.

although this does not have the unqualified support of the governments of all member states, many of which dislike centralised legislation and fear the costs, both social and financial, of radical change, it continues the trend of involving business in wider social issues. In Britain, the Conservative government's Citizen's Charter indicates the extent to which even the political party which has opposed interventionism in the past has changed in response to changing social attitudes and priorities.

From 1992 with the advent of the single market in Europe, employers must, whether they like it or not, take account of common standards on everything from working practices to the environment.

The political climate of the 1980s in Britain involved a self-conscious rolling back of the boundaries of the state. Government, which since the nineteenth century had been expanding its areas of involvement in the life of the individual and the corporation began, in many areas, to disengage. The political philosophy of the Thatcher years was one of self-help, enterprise and corporate citizenship. This latter suggested that business, particularly big business, could and should shoulder some of the responsibility for training, social programmes, financing of the arts and so on. Business felt unable to refuse. Thus Peter Morgan, then of the Institute of Directors, felt that 'the government has challenged enterprise to take on active corporate citizenship'.[7] In similar vein, Sir Adrian Cadbury, talking about the social responsibility of companies, sees large organisations as 'capable of changing the societies in which they carry out their business, for better or worse [and] governmental goals can often only be achieved through the cooperation of companies'.[8]

In one sense, this political culture encouraged companies to look out to the wider community and determine their responsibilities there. Read in another way, however, its rejection of 'dependency' and the emphasis on self-reliance and personal achievement in the enterprise culture gave rise to a new breed, the yuppies, a new vocabulary of 'golden hellos', 'loadsa money' and, according to the movie *Wall Street*, businessmen with 'ethical by-passes'. The reaction against the 'greed culture' was not long

[7] Interview with Peter Morgan, *Director*, July 1989, p. 50.
[8] Sir Adrian Cadbury, *The Company Chairman*, Fitzwilliam Publishing, 1990, p. 147.

in coming. It was parodied by one commentator in his suggestions for some new Beatitudes:

Blessed are the predators, for they shall inherit the earth.
Blessed are they which do hunger and thirst insatiably, for they shall be filled.
Blessed are the merciless, for they shall obtain their quarry.[9]

In similar mood, *The Economist* warned of a 'backlash against business', suggesting that, in the 1990s, 'the business ethic is going to be questioned, criticised, sometimes even vilified'.[10] Rejection of what were perceived to be the attitudes and values of the enterprise culture was reinforced by reactions to the various business scandals of the late 1980s such as Guinness, Blue Arrow and Barlow Clowes. The storm of indignation they provoked, not necessarily always well informed, nevertheless made business aware of its own precarious reputation and of the need to think seriously about ethical issues.

In addition to such negative pressures on business to put its house in order were social and organisational changes which encouraged companies to take a long hard look at their aims and their attitudes to employees, customers, the environment and their shareholders. Charles Handy talks about the development of flatter corporations, where layers of management have been cut out and where authority is devolved to the lowest possible level.[11] In this kind of structure, employees need to have a clear understanding of the ends and aims of their organisation and a strong sense of shared values, which can only be achieved if ethical questions have been addressed directly and openly.

In another sense, too, concern for employees is not a matter of altruism on the part of companies today. British industry is facing in the 1990s the results of the largest fall in the birth-rate this century. Between the mid-1960s and 1970s, it fell from over a million to around 700,000 a year as more couples delayed starting families or decided to have only a single child. The pill, the more liberal abortion policy introduced by the 1967 Abortion Act, and changes in women's lifestyle and working patterns

---

[9] Andrew Phillips, Opening Address to the International Conference on Business Ethics, 'A Question of Values', Wolfson College, Cambridge, July 1989, *Proceedings*, p. 12.
[10] *The Economist*, 15 April 1989, leading article.
[11] Charles Handy, *The Age of Unreason*, Century Hutchinson, 1989.

altruism –

have all contributed to births for some time now being below replacement (about 1.7 where replacement is 2).[12] By 1995, it is estimated that there will be 1.5 million fewer 16- to 24-year-olds and employers will be facing a recruitment war. Business is well aware of this development and many employers are already setting out to attract the best of the available talent.

One of the ways in which this can be done is by taking account of what people are looking for in a job and this seems to be as much or more to do with the ethos of the firm as with pay and conditions. People, especially the young, are apparently rejecting, if indeed they ever really espoused, the self-advancement culture of the past ten years. Employees, perhaps not unnaturally, want to feel proud to be a part of the enterprise for which they work, to feel that it is admired and respected, which in turn makes them feel good about themselves.[13] A recent survey of job factors which were selected as most important by employees in Britain found that top of the list came being treated with fairness and respect. Pay came only fourth.[14]

If all these trends and tendencies were not enough to encourage business to look more carefully at how its commercial aim could best be achieved, the views of shareholders themselves might have encouraged it to do so. Milton Friedman's assumption that what stockholders want is for the company to make as much money for them as possible is not necessarily backed up by business experience. As one company chairman says, 'In practice . . . shareholders have differing views on how companies should make money and on how they should distribute it. Their objectives differ and they are not confined to furthering the strictly economic role of companies.'[15] Indeed, recent developments in the area of ethical investment trusts would seem to indicate that many investors, like employees, are very keen to feel good about the firms in which they are involved. Certainly not all of them are simply after a quick financial return and they are often clear about the areas – like tobacco, alcohol, gambling, or arms – into which they do not want to put their money.

---

[12] *Social Trends*, 19, 1990, HMSO, 1990.
[13] S. Carmichael and J. Drummond, *Good Business*, Business Books, 1989, pp. 5–6.
[14] *Training and Development, Journal of the Institute of Training and Development*, November 1990, p. 20.
[15] Cadbury, *The Company Chairman*, pp. 145–6.

And if this is the negative side of shareholder attitudes, the positive is shown by the large measure of acceptance for 'corporate giving'. Barclays Bank, for example, was the object of a prolonged public campaign to have it cease doing business in South Africa. Students protested, accounts were closed and shareholdings sold. In 1986, Barclays got out of South Africa saying, 'Our customer base, particularly in the United Kingdom and the United States, was beginning to be adversely affected by our minority holding in Barclays National.'[16] At about the same time, Barclays joined the Percent Club, the organisation of leading British companies which contract to give 0.5 per cent of their profits to fund community projects. No shareholder has yet objected to this company policy.

All of these influences – from the impact of European Community legislation to the demographic imperatives – have conspired to encourage business now to look long and hard at ethical issues and priorities. This is not a preoccupation that will go away and it is therefore important that the ground on which discussion proceeds is at least staked out. Otherwise, we may all waste much time and effort reinventing the wheel: and we will, in any case, have no common language in which to communicate or common framework in terms of which to proceed.

What follows is a beginning only: it is an attempt to outline a business ethic based not, like the classical theories of moral philosophy, on notions of personal self-development but on the idea of business itself. If this at least recommends itself to business's practitioners as a suitable place to start, and allows them to see the relevance of practical ethics for their own experience, it will have served its purpose. It will then be up to them to take it forward in their business lives.

[16] Annual report and accounts, Barclays Bank, 1986. Statement by the Chairman, Sir Timothy Bevan.

The ethics of business

The secret of life is honesty and fair dealing. If you can fake that, you've got it made.

(Groucho Marx)

He was as great as a man could be without virtue.

(Lord Acton on Napoleon)

WHY ETHICS?

People in business make decisions every day which affect the rights and interests of others, both those within the business and those outside. Rights and interests are the basic stuff of ethical debate. Such decisions are made on the basis of assumptions – about the business's aims and aspirations; about what is owed to other people; about underlying values and direction. It is one of the central arguments of this book that it is better that such assumptions be made overt, so that they can be acknowledged and argued about, rather than remaining unspoken and therefore unchallenged and undiscussed.

It is sometimes suggested that business decisions are technical decisions, that is, that they are taken in the light of specific information which can be processed by means of modern business methods to give specific answers to questions of investment, divestiture, etc. On this view, financial techniques such as establishing an internal rate of return (IRR) or a pay-back in effect make the decision for us. Ethics is at best redundant, at worst misleading, diverting business from its real task of maximising profits. Yet almost all business decisions are more complex than this would suggest. They involve calculations not only of return on investment but of effects on employees, customers, the community, the environment – none of which can be reduced to simple algebra. The case for shutting down a particular operation

may be conclusive in financial terms, yet the cost in terms of
morale in the business as a whole if this were to happen, or the
needs of a local community dependent on the jobs, may ultimately
be judged more important.

Again, a particular market opportunity may be shown to be
strategically achievable by legal means. Few people would agree,
however, that this is tantamount to a decision to proceed. If
success involves heavy inducements to retailers or a campaign
of misleading advertising, the board would have to discuss a
great deal more than profit margins.

Still, the fact remains that there is some doubt about the
appropriateness of importing ethical categories into business par-
lance. Until recently, this has particularly been the case in
business schools where the norm has been to concentrate on the
'hard' disciplines, like economics, finance and accounting, which
can boast, so it is claimed, objective, quantitative methodologies.
By contrast, ethics is seen as subjective and relativistic. Yet, of
course, economics and finance are themselves riddled with value
assumptions – about rational economic man or perfect market
information, for example – and depend for their certainty on the
construction of a world where 'ceteris' are always 'paribus'! When
it comes to the scrappiness of the real world, a world of imperfect
information and unpredictable human action, these disciplines
can tell us only a very limited amount. Their methodologies
perhaps give their practitioners delusions of grandeur, the belief
that their application can solve real problems, when they are
often more akin to the technique of the drunk looking for a
dropped coin underneath a lamp-post, not because that is where
it fell but because that is the only place there is any light.

There is concern too, about discussing business ethics in the
academic context, dismissing it as merely a 'consciousness-raising'
activity, encouraging managers to 'be good', rather than a rigorous, analytical tool.[1] But raising people's consciousness about the
importance of spelling out values and standards amounts to a
great deal more than simple protestations about being against
sin. It involves attempting to develop acceptable priorities and
frameworks within which complex and often contradictory claims

[1] T. Dunfee and D. Robertson, Integrating ethics into the business school curriculum,
Journal of Business Ethics, November 1988, pp. 847-59.

can be assessed. It may also begin to break down artificial barriers between theory and practice, whereby ethical arguments are assigned to the former category, while business is placed firmly in the latter. Business practice, the making of business judgements, however, clearly includes assumptions about values, standards and priorities – all of which may involve ethical issues. Ethics is not simply a glorified intellectual game, of no practical relevance. We become moral individuals, as Aristotle says, by practice; good at being truthful by habitually telling the truth; becoming characteristically honest by trying always not to be dishonest.[2] There is nothing abstract or grandiose about business ethics understood in this sense; it is simply another tool, not unlike Discounted Cash Flow or the Capital Asset Pricing Model, to help the practical man or woman deal with the endlessly recurring moral dilemmas of business life.

Again, the relativism and subjectivism which are seen as endemic to ethical discussion seem to some to imprison it within a specific culture or even a specific transaction. Our moral frameworks, it is sometimes said, are the product of our time and place and are not necessarily appropriately moved from one culture to another. This makes them particularly suspect at a time when business sees itself as international. Can there be a 'global ethic'? Or is one man's 'bribe' always going to be another man's 'commission'? The point here surely is that, since cultural differences do as a matter of fact exist, they must be faced and dealt with. They cannot be simply ignored, and stigmatising ethics for pointing them out is like shooting the messenger because you don't like the inconvenience of the message. In fact, in no society is bribery accepted as morally good and some companies have made important strides in developing an international value system, proscribing certain activities world-wide. Slow and difficult as this may be, it surely has to be attempted.

There is a connection between our perception of the world and the way in which we make decisions in the world. If managers believe that they are and ought to be rational egoists, concerned only with maximising profit, they will take decisions accordingly. If, on the other hand, they are aware of moral

---

[2] Aristotle, *Nicomachean Ethics*, trans. D. Ross, Oxford University Press, World's Classics Paperback, 1988.

theories and social policies that affect their own societies and the wider world, they will be likely to make rather different and perhaps more sophisticated judgements.

Again, to raise and discuss ethical issues in the business context is not only to give managers more confidence that they have something to say here; it is also to legitimise such issues for them, to make them a natural part of the agenda which feels neither alien nor out of place. In this context, business ethics quite self-consciously sets out to counteract what has been called 'the moral muteness of managers' whereby, although they may personally recognise that ethical principles bear on management, business people have little or no experience of talking about them.[3] Consequently, they feel embarrassed and inadequate in this area; they cannot find the words and therefore ignore the arguments, or experience moral talk as uncomfortable, out of place or even counter-productive.

In the not very distant past, to ask not only how a particular project would affect the bottom line but what impact it would have on the local community might have been seen as a rather tangential enquiry. Now this would be an immediate concern of many of those making such decisions. Business has, in other words, become more complex and more aware of the inevitable social, cultural and moral ramifications of its decisions. Because of this, business schools which fail to raise such wider issues as part of their core curriculum are failing their students in a central way. They leave them marooned on an island of their own techniques, still believing that correct decisions will spring ready-made out of a personal computer running a spreadsheet model. In the real world, judgements are much harder to make and an understanding of wider obligations and commitments – to employees, customers, shareholders and so on – is essential.

Once this framework of the many constituencies of business is accepted, of course, the possibility of conflict between interests becomes clear. There is no problem about what to do in situations where everybody gains, where the situation can be what economists call Pareto optimal; the trouble starts where hard choices

[3] F. Bird and J. Waters, The moral muteness of managers, *California Management Review*, vol. 32, no. 1, 1989, p. 73.

have to be made about winners and losers. Ethical problems arise where such judgements have to be made.

IS EVERYTHING ETHICS?

On the face of it, the whole area of business and commerce seems alive with ethical issues concerning, for example, the rights of individuals or groups or the protection of the environment. At one level, this is so and much of the rest of this book is devoted to identifying and elucidating many of these issues. However, it is important to be clear that this is not a statement of either theoretical or practical imperialism! It is not to say that ethics is everything or everything is ethics. Let us take some examples from the history of ethical theory. Thomas Aquinas talks about the need to clarify the action which we are trying to identify.[4] Is this action, he suggests we should ask ourselves, moral, immoral or simply amoral? As he points out, some actions – stroking one's chin, for example – can hardly be classified within an ethical framework. At the least, he says, we need to specify the action in terms of its description, its intention and its context. Is this a murder or an execution, for example? What is the intended outcome? What is the situation of the key participants and how will they contribute to the action and its outcome? It is always worth bearing this background in mind before making assertions about the morality or otherwise of complicated economic and commercial activity. If an activity is, say, against the law or contrary to an established management–union agreement, then calling it 'unethical' may not add anything very useful to its description. In other words, it may be best not described in ethical terms at all.

This is not to say, however, that being ethical can be subsumed under the heading of simply obeying the law. The ethical corporation is not defined as one which abides by legislation; ethics is not merely compliance. Rather, the ethical corporation will normally obey the law as the basic minimum response in any problematic situation in which it finds itself. But it will do more than this: it will be aware of its obligations to those inside and

[4] *Basic Writings of St Thomas Aquinas*, ed. A. C. Pegis, New York Publications, 1948.

outside the company who are affected by its actions and whose interests will be reflected in its values.

Another useful model is that offered by Niccolò Machiavelli. The author of the notorious *Prince* may seem a bizarre choice when it comes to discussing questions of morality. However, he was not, of course, simply the predictable amoralist of the 'old Nick' stereotype; he has some interesting things to say about different modes of behaviour. Talking about politics and morality, Machiavelli claims that politics is an autonomous form of activity.[5] Without denying the force of the moral law, he suggests that rulers and saints do not, indeed cannot, have the same aims and ends. However, morality is not the sole framework of value, only of moral value. To take an ethical stance in a political or commercial situation may be to misidentify the real issues as they affect people's lives. It may be to make what philosophers sometimes call a category-mistake. It may also be the coward's way out, leaving us with the comfortable feeling of being beyond reproach because we have done 'the right thing' but ignoring longer term consequences. Those who need to take the moral line all the time, to the exclusion of everything else, should not be in politics or business. As the American president Harry Truman said, 'If you can't stand the heat, stay out of the kitchen.' Hard decisions have to be made in the real world and they should not be confused with moral imperatives. The attitude which sees ethics as the answer to all questions in business is thus perhaps only the mirror image of that which believes that business decisions are technical decisions. The positions are equally simplistic, the one assuming that we merely need to assert 'the right', the other to derive the rate of return, and nothing will be problematic any more.

The Machiavellian line, which tries to drive a wedge between moral and other forms of activity can, of course, be a dangerous argument which leads to amorality. In suggesting that everything is not ethics, it could imply that some things never have an ethical dimension – business, for example, which might be supposed to be driven by other criteria and in which ethical standards have no place.

The modern Machiavellian in this context is, it seems, Milton

[5] N. Machiavelli, *The Prince*, trans with intro. George Bull, Penguin Books, 1981.

Friedman. In a now famous essay, he claims that the suggestion that business should have social and ethical aims and aspirations is 'a fundamentally subversive doctrine'.[6] This is because 'corporate officials [have no] social responsibility other than to make as much for their stockholders as possible'.[7] At one level, this may be seen as a profoundly immoral statement: make as much as you can in any way you can. Even if the suggestion is softened to exclude law-breaking, it still apparently leaves much to be desired in ethical terms.

However, Friedman is not simply being a banal immoralist; he may just want to point out, rather as Machiavelli did, that there are, in this sophisticated modern world, many different forms of social activity. One of these, but only one, is business. Business people are not politicians or social workers; corporations are not government departments or philanthropic institutions; ICI is neither the Department of the Environment nor Oxfam. The ends of business are commercial ends; business is there to make profits; if it is not making profits, it is out of business. Other social institutions exist to look after our immortal souls, our physical health, the improvement of our minds and so on. It is to give business dangerously exaggerated powers to suggest that, in addition to doing its job of making profits, it should also make our social or moral decisions for us. Business institutions or their boards of directors are not elected by the public; where, therefore, does this power come from to pursue social ends, to decide on everything from employee health to community environmental policy? The answer is that it has no legitimate basis; it is the hijacking of social and political power by private interests and, as such, it had better be opposed. Business should stick to its knitting, make money and pay its taxes, which can then be used for social ends, as these are decided by the properly elected representatives of the people, the government of the day.

So far, so good for Friedman, if this is indeed what he is saying. His argument disposes of the more simplistic notions of the relationship between ethics and business. There is still the

---

[6] M. Friedman, The social responsibility of business is to increase its profits, *New York Times* magazine, 13 September 1970, p. 87.
[7] Friedman, Social responsibility.

question, however, of whether that relationship exists at some more complex level.

For example, the commercial world has always claimed a 'business ethic', a way of operating which is considered acceptable within that context. 'My word is my bond' was the basis of commercial dealings long before the development of the City Takeover Panel or the Monopolies and Mergers Commission. Business ethics have, in one sense, amounted to the progressive articulation of that simple code of conduct – sticking to a bargain once struck. As commercial dealings have become more and more complex, however, so the rules of play have become ever more specific. At the same time, business has become more and more the subject of public scrutiny. We live in a society where deference is no longer the basis of socially acceptable behaviour, but where experts and professionals of all kinds are expected to justify their views and decisions. Those in business, like their counterparts in the professions, are asked increasingly to explain what they are doing and why they are doing it.

This is a relatively recent development: at the height of the Industrial Revolution, nobody questioned the morality of business. It created wealth, and the Protestant ethic reinforced, if it did not actually produce, the spirit of capitalism.[8] To be commercially successful then was very nearly the same thing as to be socially responsible. However, in more recent times, there has developed what one commentator has called 'an ambivalent moral attitude to industry'.[9] Business needs to prove its ethical credentials, and social responsibility may now include anything from doing an environmental audit to sponsoring *Figaro* at Glyndebourne.

The complexity and changeability of modern business too, encouraged by Big Bang, 24-hour trading and so on, have also changed attitudes within as well as outside the business community. Our technology, our capacity to outsmart ourselves, has sometimes outstripped our ethical framework. What price (literally) has 'My word is my bond' when the frontiers of

---

[8] See for example, R. Tawney, *Religion and the Rise of Capitalism*, Penguin, 1961. Also, M. Weber, The protestant ethic and the spirit of capitalism, trans. A. Henderson and T. Parsons, in *Collected Essays*, The Free Press, 1947.

[9] Kenneth Adams, Changing British attitudes, *RSA Journal*, vol. 138, November, 1990, p. 827.

possibility change almost from day to day? Something of the same dilemma has developed in the area of biotechnology, where rapid changes in what is possible have left traditional standards beached and often irrelevant; not because practitioners are careless of ethical issues but because the parameters within which they view these activities keep moving. Are surrogate motherhood or embryo experimentation ethically acceptable? There are respectable arguments on both sides. The painful fact is that, in a very short space of time, these things have become technically and practically feasible and confront us with entirely new moral dilemmas. As moral philosophers are wont to say, 'ought' implies 'can'. In other words, for something to be morally required (or proscribed) it must be practically possible. On the other hand, 'can' doesn't necessarily imply 'ought': because we have the capacity to do something, in that the technology allows it, does not give us moral *carte blanche*. At the least, then, if they are to be recognised as constantly relevant, basic business values such as 'My word is my bond' have to be constantly reworked and progressively rearticulated in changing social and commercial circumstances.

THE NATURE OF BUSINESS ETHICS

If not everything is ethics, can we define its precise nature? We have established that ethics is not the same as compliance with the law. Indeed, compliance is neither necessary nor sufficient in all cases for action to be ethical. Business will generally be presumed, however, to obey the law if only because it depends for its very existence on the law being upheld. The establishment of corporations, the notion of limited liability, as well as the upholding of contracts and property rights, are all examples of the dependence of business on the law. A business which disobeys the law is likely to undermine its own existence.

But what if the law is a bad law? What if a business were required, by law, to discriminate in employment against certain sections of the population – women or Jews, for example?[10] How

---

[10] The examples are not, of course, fanciful. Thomas Keneally's book, *Schindler's Ark* (Hodder and Stoughton, 1982) traces the outcomes of legalised discrimination against Jewish workers; and until well after the Second World War women in many jobs were unprotected by law when forced to resign from work on marriage.

far we should go in opposing a bad law is a question for political philosophy and not for business ethics, but the general issue may impinge on the specific business context.[11] What then? Should business comply? Generally the answer is yes, for the reason, given above, that business owes its existence to the law and the framework of confidence which the law allows. This is not to say that business need sit by and do nothing. The normal channels of protest open to citizens in a democracy – writing to the press, lobbying MPs, ministers and civil servants and so on – are open to business and all the more powerfully available because of the importance of business in so many political calculations.

But if all of this is to no avail and business still feels that the law is counter-productive to its aim, what then? The law forbidding most Sunday trading in England and Wales was a case in point. It was not only anachronistic and irrelevant as far as most people were concerned, but was also confused and in possible contravention of the European Treaty of Rome.[12] Yet even in such a case, many retailers were rightly aware of the possible repercussions of breaking the law. The problem was not fundamentally about the outcomes of conviction: local authorities, who had prosecuting responsibilities were loath to get involved and, even when they occasionally did, fines were small. But the retailers were aware of the damage which might be done to their credibility, not just with customers but with employees, suppliers and indeed the government. There was an awareness that, although the law as it stood might not have been in the long-term interests of the company, neither necessarily was breaking the law.[13] Significantly, those who decided to do so were quick to point out that it was the confused state of the law which led them to their decision, which they hoped would put pressure on the government to clarify the position speedily.

---

[11] The issue of compliance or otherwise with an immoral law is dealt with at least as far back as Sophocles' *Antigone*, who claims, 'The order did not come from god. Justice/ That dwells with the gods below, knows no such law' (451–2).

[12] See the statement made in the House of Commons by the then minister, Angela Rumbold, Hansard, 27 November 1991.

[13] There was some uncertainty about the profitability of Sunday opening and whether it generated sufficient in the way of incremental sales to cover the costs of seven-day trading. See e.g. Sunday trading could prove a costly mistake, *The Independent*, 7 January 1992.

The other side of the coin is where ethical considerations may seem to require a business to do *more* than merely comply with the law. If a business made informal agreements with its employees on, say, pensions or redundancy payments, and the law was then clarified to require lower settlements, the merely legal path might not be the ethical one. If expectations had genuinely been raised and agreements assumed, the business would have to consider its position carefully; not just in terms of whether its relationships with employees, present and future, were at risk if it were thought to have reneged on its initial position, but whether this was an ethical action in the circumstances. In general, then, business should be presumed to obey the law and honour its contracts, not because this is *the same as* being ethical but because the law is the context within which business activity itself is created and maintained and because the aim of business is normally most likely to be achieved within that context. But ethics is still not the same as compliance: it can be more, although it will not normally be less.

Just as ethics is not the same as compliance with the law, so it is not the same as religion. Historically, it is true that many ethical principles are associated with religious beliefs and most of the major religions enjoin similar basic moral values – not lying, cheating, stealing but being honest, just, reliable and so on. But the aim of business is not the same as the aim of religion. A 'Jewish business' or a 'Christian business' would suggest that religious aims took priority over commercial business ones – a confusion in terms. A 'business' which had a religious aim would simply not be a business. This is not to say that some businesses do not take aspects of the moral codes associated with, say, Christianity or Judaism and make them central to their *business* values. For example, care and concern for employees is central to Marks and Spencer's business culture and this is often said to derive from the Jewish family values of the founders of the business. Of course, these values have proved to be commercially relevant as well as being ethically sound. If, however, Marks and Spencer had insisted, on religious grounds, that all female employees had their heads shaved (rather than, as they do, their hair done) they would probably not have inspired the same enthusiasm among their workforce.

Individual businesses can be ethical without subscribing to

any particular religion. Religious values reflect the 'eternal verit-
ies': they may be seen through the lenses of Islam or Judaism
or Christianity or humanism but they are not identical with any
of them.

IF IT'S GOOD FOR BUSINESS, IS IT REALLY ETHICAL?

Although some businessmen will argue that being ethical with
their staff, customers, suppliers, shareholders and the local community, costs them money in training, in quality, in not cutting
corners and so on, many now say that good ethics is good
business. Lindsay Owen-Jones, Chairman of L'Oréal, sums up
this latter attitude when he says, 'Business ethics are not a
restraint that companies impose on themselves for simply moral
reasons. Doing business honestly is also the most efficient way
to do business long-term.'[14] This view was expressed too by
the Chairman of the United States Securities and Exchange
Commission, John Shad, when he gave $10 million to Harvard
Business School for the teaching of ethics: 'I believe ethics pays',
he said. 'It's smart to be ethical.' And the great guru of self-
confident management success, Tom Peters, talks in his latest
book about the need to 'demand total integrity'.[15]

If the ethical corporation, by being ethical, attracts the right
people, keeps customers, suppliers and shareholders happy with
its performance, creates and maintains a good corporate identity
and altogether finds ethics gives it a competitive edge, is this
ethical? Or, as Jack Mahoney, Professor of Business Ethics at
the London Business School, asks, is to be ethical in these
circumstances to 'do the right deed for the wrong reason'?[16]

A number of points need to be made here. To begin with,
honesty is almost certainly the best policy and ethical operations
the most productive, if you intend to be in the marketplace over
a long period of time. You will then have, or be in process of
building, a name and reputation, neither of which you can afford
to lose. You cannot take dubious short cuts if they may leave
you with no long-term business. Lord Laing (then Sir Hector

---

[14] Interview with Lindsay Owen-Jones, *The McKinsey Quarterly*, Autumn 1989, p. 41.
[15] Tom Peters, *Thriving on Chaos*, Pan Books, 1989, pp. 519ff.
[16] Lecture series on Business and Social Responsibility. *The Role of Business in Society*,
published by Gresham College, 1989.

Laing and Chairman of United Biscuits), introducing his firm's statement of values, makes this clear in the opening paragraph: 'No element of management responsibility is more important . . . than to provide for the future of the company . . . We will therefore never attempt to maximise short-term profitability at the expense of action necessary for the survival of the business in the long term.'[17]

It would have been a fair guess, even before reading this statement, that United Biscuits fully intends to survive beyond the end of the week or even the year and its ethics is part of that strategy. But what if your business (this week) is selling 'solid gold' necklaces for £10 apiece in Oxford Street? Your reputation may not seem too important; you have no employees; your only shareholder is your wife whose housekeeping you used to buy the stock and you've paid her with some of the merchandise; your customers will, with luck, never see you again, and anyway, what did they expect for £10? It is hardly surprising that you feel no need to join the Percent Club.

Good ethics is good business in the long term. It is probably also the largest companies which see the biggest returns from a clear ethical statement, if only because they have the most to lose. Very large companies are in the public eye. They are endlessly commented on and their activities, social and political as well as commercial and financial, are discussed and noted. It is they who have spent time and money building up their brands and honing their corporate identity (not for nothing is there a debate about including brands on the balance sheet); it is they, therefore, who cannot allow the assiduously cultivated relationships with their many constituents to be damaged. This does not, however, allow smaller operations to act according to a different set of moral values. For unless they have no regard for their future, like the Oxford Street pedlar, they are subject to the predominant business ethos where the exemplary culture, as one might call it, is set by the big barons. No self-respecting business, however small, wants to be regarded as dishonest, uncaring of its employees or customers or obsessively short-termist. It can no longer evade its responsibilities without giving the impression of being in a precarious position and consequently losing confidence.

To return to the moral question: can business practice claim to

---

[17] United Biscuits, Ethics and Operating Principles, December 1987, p. 3.

be ethical if it is advantageous to the organisation? First of all, we need to dispense with the Judaeo-Christian association of moral good with suffering. The suggestion here is that only if the medicine tastes bad will it do good; only if you do what you do not want to do but feel is your *duty* are you really playing for moral stakes. This deontological approach, the kind of line taken by Kant, for example, makes an absolute distinction between morality and prudence: to do something because you believe the outcome will be beneficial is quite different from doing it because you believe it is your duty to do it, and only the latter can be properly described as ethical.

But good *actions* are not made any less good because they are in one's interest. Business ethics is concerned to produce certain outcomes in business, that is, to encourage good *actions*. It is these, rather than the motives of the individuals involved, which are of interest here. Only if we were concerned to evaluate business people as moral agents would we be interested primarily in motives rather than actions.

There need therefore be no absolute disjunction between moral action and outcomes favourable to the agent or others. Indeed, the two may stand in a close, if convoluted, relationship. Again, to realise that an action is advantageous is not necessarily to do it only because it is advantageous: one may also do it because it is right. One might also be aware that it is advantageous largely because it is perceived to be right but this need not mean that one does it simply in order to be seen to be right.[18] Indeed, if a company value statement, like a personal ethical code, were pursued strictly as a public relations exercise, it would be overtly thin and hollow. People – employees, customers, shareholders – would quickly become aware of this and the whole exercise would probably be counter-productive. The organisation which thinks it is cleverly using 'ethics' as a thinly disguised piece of corporate relations is not being ethical, but neither will it gain the rewards of an ethical approach.

IS THE ETHICS OF BUSINESS THE BUSINESS OF ETHICS?

As I have said, business decisions are not merely technical decisions which can be given clear and simple financial answers.

---

[18] I am indebted here to Jack Mahoney's clear discussion of 'mixed motives' in his lecture series mentioned above.

They are mostly multidimensional and require a framework of priorities and values within which they can be analysed. Business and ethics are not two separate and alien structures; neither does ethics seek to colonise business priorities in an illegitimate way. But, as all human action, including that in business, involves judgement, so those involved in business should be aware of their priorities and values. An ethical framework does not *make* business decisions but it allows such decisions to be clarified. Moral philosophy has never pretended to solve our individual moral dilemmas and a book on business ethics is not and cannot be an easy reference system for solving those of modern business. On the other hand, it is only by acknowledging that business is frequently faced with competing claims and apparently incompatible demands that necessary choices can be made. To do nothing is still to make a choice.

In one sense, ethics provides no answers; but it does offer the structures and frameworks within which problems can be examined. Without a moral framework, we lurch from problem to problem, from one *ad hoc* solution to another, forever reinventing the wheel. Business ethics can help us make our way through living dilemmas, theory and practice can come together and the apparent ivory tower of philosophical analysis can provide a basis for practical moral action. For this to be possible, however, we need a clear view of the *aim* of business and chapter 2 will therefore try to determine what business is *for* and how this affects its ethical operation.

2

The nature and aim of business

> Man exploits man and sometimes the other way round.
> (Woody Allen)

> Every individual ... intends only his own gain and he is
> in this ... led by an invisible hand to promote an end
> which is no part of his intention.
> (Adam Smith, *The Wealth of Nations*)

Any investigation of business ethics must begin by looking not
only at ethics and the ways in which it relates to business, but
at business itself. If we want to discover how and in what ways
values can underpin business decisions, we have first to be clear
what form business activity itself takes: what, in other words,
are its aims and aspirations. As Aristotle tells us, it helps in
hitting the mark to know what it is you are aiming for.[1] The
idea is so basic, of such stunning simplicity, that it is easy to
underestimate its importance. Success in business may involve
the evolution of strategies of considerable complexity; but logically
prior to debates on the value of strategic planning or financial
control has to be the question of the aim of business itself. It is
unlikely you will hit the mark, regardless of the sophistication
of your plan or the extent of your skill, if you do not know,
absolutely and unswervingly, what your target is.

In these terms, a fundamental question of business ethics is
'What is business for?' This is not merely a semantic exercise,
for it is crucial to clear decision-making in business that business
itself can be distinguished from other superficially similar kinds
of organisation. To identify this 'ideal type' of business for purposes of definition is not to suggest that business has some kind

[1] Aristotle, *The Nicomachean Ethics*.

26

of honorific status or that organisations that are not businesses, such as governmental or charitable ones, are in some sense inferior. They are not: they simply do not share the purely business aim. As I shall argue, business is a quite limited and specific form of activity, and asking the question about its nature and aim forces us to be explicit about what characterises it and differentiates it from other kinds of organisation. It also encourages us to think through the whole question of what is relevant to the business purpose.

It might be argued that we have misidentified our subject here right at the start and that we ought to be looking at the aim or purpose of 'the corporation' rather than that of 'business', a less specific concept. Yet business is the generic form of which the corporation is only one type. It is not the legal form of limited liability which is of interest to us but the kind of activity of which that legal form is just one, albeit important, variety. Although we will often talk of owners as shareholders, it is business rather than simply the corporation which is our key subject, because ethical concerns often arise as a result of the objectives of the activity and not just the specific legal framework.

PUBLIC ATTITUDES TO BUSINESS

Before we begin to ask specifically about the aim of business in general, or the aim of a particular business, we need to understand the changing public attitude to business and how this has influenced business's view of itself.

In the last century, the business community was secure in its own role, certain that it contributed to the common good by the creation of wealth and the expansion of opportunities. Of course, there were always those who denigrated industry as squalid and self-seeking and 'trade' as socially unacceptable but the achievements of business were there for all to see in the progressive increase in the standard of living. And public attitudes to business largely reflected, and perhaps reinforced, this self-esteem until around the 1960s, when things began to change. In 1962, the public confidence level in business was still about 70 per cent; by the early 1980s it had fallen to 19 per cent.[2] By 1989,

---

[2] J. Gray, *Managing the Corporate Image*, Quorum Books, 1986, p. 18.

a Mori poll surveying public attitudes to different social groups found that only local councillors and estate agents were less respected than company directors.[3]

Against this background, it is hardly surprising that, when the question about the purpose or end of business is raised, it can evoke a certain uneasiness among business people. Sensing a general hostility to the whole area, they will naturally try to counter it by denying that business is corrupt, self-seeking and socially irresponsible and emphasising its ethical awareness and social concern. But in so doing, they may sometimes be led into confusion about and even misrepresentation of their own priorities and ends.

Yet there are a number of reasons why business people are often less than keen to identify their aim purely commercially. To begin with, the stark statement in terms such as Milton Friedman's that the aim of business is simply to increase its profits is unlikely, as it stands, to win many friends in a society increasingly concerned with consumer and employee rights. The *Zeitgeist* seems to have swung against the profit motive. As a recent survey of business schools put it, for the 1990s, 'greed is out, ethics is in'.[4] In this context, ethics appears as the new badge of acceptability for business.

Again, it is quite understandable that people in business do not want to be thought of as unconcerned about and unresponsive to society's wider needs. And realistically, the interests of many people other than shareholders – employees, customers, suppliers, government, the local, national and international community – are clearly important to business. They are stakeholders in the business and, it could be argued, have to be taken into account in the business aim.

This wide-ranging set of interests, then, begins to suggest a much broader business remit than simply a concern with its own profitability. And indeed it is surely true that businesses depend for their success on far more than just their equity capital. It is

[3] Mori poll conducted for the *Sunday Times*, August 1989.
[4] The best professional schools in America, US News and World Report, March 1990.

often said, for example, that businesses are no better than their people. It is employees who make businesses work, who add value, who create the strategies and deliver the goods. Similarly, without customers there can be no business, only a service nobody wants or an accumulating inventory. And one can go on in similar vein through the various groups who in their different ways contribute to the business.

Viewed thus, Milton Friedman's focus on profit as the sole aim of business begins to look rather less convincing. He seems simply to have singled out one stakeholder, the shareholder, and suggested that this is the only one who counts. If, however, as is clearly the case, business relies on more than just providers of capital, does it therefore have a duty to do more than make profits? To go back to our original question, is it now a part of the *aim* of business to take care of its employees, customers and the local community?

WHAT BUSINESS IS NOT

The short and simple answer is no. The aim of business is, as I have said, a commercial aim: business exists to provide goods and services in order to make profits; if it is not making profits, its very existence will soon be in question. However, in seeking to provide the conditions for profit-making, businesses will, of course, ignore staff, customer and community interests at their peril. Though businesses do not exist primarily so that their employees can be fulfilled human beings or so that their suppliers can feel loved, they have come to realise that decently treated employees and appropriately appreciated suppliers generally perform better.

But it is important to get things the right way round. It is not the *aim* of business to provide personal fulfilment and spiritual development, or a clean environment, or full employment. Businesses are concerned with the self-development of their staff and the interests of their other stakeholders only to the extent that these contribute to the aim of the business, which is the creation of long-term value for the owners of the business.

Other social institutions exist to look after our souls, our physical well-being and the improvement of our minds. Such institutions, like churches and educational establishments, may well seek to create appropriate financial returns. Unlike businesses, however, they do so not as their main aim, but in order to fulfil their primary spiritual or educational objectives. To fail to make the distinction of priority of aim, or to collapse the one into the other, is to be fundamentally confused and confusing.

BUSINESS IS NOT THE WHOLE OF LIFE

Looked at like this, the ethical and social responsibility of business is less a business aim than a part of business strategy, a way of determining direction and creating and maintaining structures which enhance performance. A business's responsibility to its employees, for example, is not to fulfil them existentially but to help them achieve what the business asks of them. This means providing them not simply with proper training, but also with a culture of trust and decency, freedom and support.

However, it is important to recognise that business is not the whole of life. It is not there to be a substitute for family, school, club or church. One of the crucial differences between capitalism and communism, for example, is precisely that capitalism allows a distinction to be made between the public and the private, between what is personal and what is political. This is not a distinction that communism (at least of the Marxist variety) permits. For communism is not only an economic system but a moral theory. It is a total system within which everything is assumed to work towards the achievement of the classless society and the production and development of 'socialist individuals'. The pursuit and achievement of economic strength and of human fulfilment are believed to be one and the same thing. As Lenin has it, morality is pursued in the pursuit of the Revolution. And, one can add, the Revolution is pursued in the establishment of economic strength.

Under this system, everything other than economics – law, politics, art and morality – is thus derivative. All are 'superstructural', growing out of the economic 'substructure' they are mere reflections of the means of production, distribution and exchange. Indeed, a large part of what we mean by 'totalitarian' is that such systems commit all their centrally controlled resources to the achievement of a single, unified vision of what is claimed to be the just and the good. There is a certain irony in the fact that, as Eastern Europe dismantles communism and lurches to embrace capitalism, the market societies of the West should often be so unclear about their own aims and values that they fail to make this distinction between the aim of business and the meaning of life. The capitalist concern with people as employees or customers is not exactly the same as the communist concern with the forging of human personality. Nor should it be, because capitalism is not totalitarian. It does not and should not pretend that business activities necessarily produce spiritual fulfilment or even cradle-to-grave direction. To suggest that business should encompass these aims is not to be 'ethical' or 'socially responsible' but merely confused. Economics – and business – is not all there is to life.

And unless this distinction is explicitly made, there is a danger, as one commentator puts it, of 'overloading business with social expectations to such an extent that it may be hampered in its actual business activities, which must surely be its primary *raison d'être*'.[5] The most fundamental concern of those who want to see ethics taken into account and in its proper place in business must be to identify accurately the business aim and to keep any creeping imperialism at bay by constantly bearing in mind what business is for. As Charles Handy has said in another context, 'it is the organisation's job to deliver; it is not its job to be everyone's alternative community, providing meaning and work for all for life'.[6]

THE AIM OF BUSINESS

So, what *is* the aim of business? Essentially, business aims to make profits by selling its goods and services so as to make money for the owners of the business, to maximise the return on their investment in the long run. In the process, it will have to consider its relationships with a variety of groups who have a stake in the business, and in whose interests the business correspondingly has its stake.

[5] J. Mahoney, *Teaching Business Ethics in the UK, Europe and the USA: A Comparative Study*, Athlone, 1991.
[6] C. Handy, *The Age of Unreason*, Century Hutchinson, 1989.

This will, of course, only make sense if the business sees itself
as having a future beyond the end of the week. It is possible to
ignore stakeholders, to sell the tawdry to the gullible, but only
if you do not depend on the repeat business. Most businesses,
however, assume some degree of longevity, if not eternal life,
and are therefore dependent on the creation of loyalty and good-
will just as much as they are on controlling costs or increasing
margins. I will argue, then, that this requirement to make a
return for shareholders is a defining characteristic of business.
Where an enterprise aims at this return, it is properly called a
business; where it does not, it may be a perfectly legitimate
enterprise of another kind, but a business it is not.

It is certainly true that other forms of organisation exist where
individuals join together, as they do in business, to promote their
joint interests. A tennis club, for example, or the Society for the
Protection of Rural England or Oxfam all exist to advance and
protect the interests of their members. Very often, too, the members of such organisations put up money to support its existence
and encourage its growth and success. Such subscriptions or
donations may seem a bit like share purchase; they register an
interest and they bring, in many cases, voting rights at Annual
General Meetings. What they do not produce, however, is a
dividend or a financial return on the money given. In the case
of business investment, on the other hand, the expectation of the
return is the prime, and often sole, reason for buying into the
enterprise. Investors do not buy shares in an oil business because
they approve of oil or because they want to register moral support
for the commodity or because they think it is a worthy sector.
They buy because there are, they believe, good returns in oil
and it enhances their portfolio.

So far, so good. Business is characterised by its aim, as Aristotle
suggests to us, and this purpose is the maximisation of shareholder returns. It is a compellingly simple and straightforward
formula but it needs refining just a little. To begin with, shareholder return suggests financial return, normally in the form of
dividends. However, it is sometimes argued that dividends may
not be the only form of return; that retained earnings, for
example, are of equal value to shareholders. Indeed, there is a
long-standing debate in finance departments of business schools
on whether payment of dividends should really be necessary for

shareholders to be satisfied.[7] Since the retention of earnings increases capital gain, then it is argued, that increase has, in theory, exactly the same value to shareholders as payment of a dividend. Our original definition of the purpose of business as being the maximisation of shareholder *returns* may be more accurately identified as maximisation of shareholder *value*.

If it is accepted that value may not be confined to dividend returns, is it possible that value could be seen as not necessarily financial at all? If the owners get value in terms of a service, say, or in terms of the pride they take in being part of an organisation with a social mission or the power they believe this brings them, this could be seen as value to them. This would certainly broaden our definition to include as businesses organisations like Traidcraft or the BBC. It would also accommodate some of the apparent aims of business in other parts of the world. Japanese business, for example, expects as part of its role to take on retired public officials. The owners of the business may get value from the delivery of this social function.[8] But in widening the notion of value to beyond financial value, we lose the distinction which we have made between business and other forms of organisation. Charities, on this account, could be seen as giving value to their 'owners' by protecting rural England, say, or preserving ancient monuments.

But in businesses, and certainly in corporations where there are fiduciary relationships between directors and owners, the aim of the business is by definition a commercial one, as the value sought by owners is explicitly a financial one. This is not to say that all organisations which claim to be businesses will act as businesses all the time but it is important to be able to make the distinction.

On this analysis, the public sector – the health service, educational services, the BBC and so on, are not businesses. This is not to say that they should not be run in a business-like way or properly managed but they are 'not for profit' and their aims are different from those of business.[9]

---

[7] See, for example, R. Brealey and S. Myers, *Principles of Corporate Finance*, McGraw-Hill, 1988, pp. 362–5.

[8] See *The Economist*, 2 February 1991.

[9] For an excellent discussion of public sector management in these terms, see M. Starks, *Not for profit, not for sale*, *Policy Journals*, 1991.

The notion of maximising shareholder value should perhaps be specified still more precisely if it is to be coherent as the central aim of business. A business might, for example, do something which would maximise value today but leave it high and dry tomorrow. It would not thereby have fulfilled its purpose as a business. Without, at this stage, getting into a discussion of the complex and thorny issue of short-termism (which I deal with in chapter 5), a certain longevity must be declared as part of the business aim.

Adding all this together, then, business, as defined by its purpose, is involved in maximising long-term owner value.

AN ALTERNATIVE PARADIGM?

One might argue, however, that business cannot be just about making profits. After all, profits are not an end in themselves; they have to be used for something. Some profits will, of course, probably be reinvested in the business, which starts the cycle again. Some will be distributed to shareholders, who may use their dividends as they wish – further stock in the company, for example, or a foreign holiday or charitable donations. But this understanding of profits as means to other things does not invalidate the notion of business outlined above. Generation of profits may quite reasonably be the end of the business, while profits themselves remain the means to other ends for shareholders.

However, there is an alternative paradigm sometimes suggested which, if accepted, is undermining of the profit maximisation view. This says that, whatever it may have been in the past, *modern* business is not just about profit-making. Because of its power, business is inexorably drawn into a social role in areas where social policy cannot be adequately pursued without its participation and co-operation: examples are training, pensions, health schemes, environmental protection and a host of others. Those concerns have become, according to this claim, a part of the business aim and not something extraneous to it.

It clearly is the case that modern business is involved, through its employees, shareholders, customers and community contacts, in many such social schemes but this does not alter the fundamental and defining business aim. Making profits is still what business, as business, is fundamentally about and this does not change over time and place. However, making profits is, and is understood to be, a complicated process in complex modern societies. The ways of achieving the aim will change to take account not only of changing technology but of changing attitudes and expectations, and having concern for good 'corporate citizenship' may well be part of the strategy of a successful business. But this is not the same as to say that these various contributors to the success – or failure – of business are themselves a part of the business *aim*. That they may affect the pursuit of that aim is not in question and they need therefore to be kept constantly in mind by business people. The aim still remains the maximisation of owner value.

WHAT IS THE NATURE AND AIM OF *THIS* BUSINESS?

Sometimes situations which appear to be dominated by ethical questions are revealed as primarily involving basic commercial considerations when the nature and aim of the particular business is looked at. Should Chocbar Ltd buy an inefficient neighbouring distribution firm, sack their employees in an area of high unemployment and reorganise the operation for their own use? Logically prior to any agonising over the firm's position on redundancy packages or their relations with the local community should undoubtedly be an enquiry about the nature of Chocbar's business. They have a niche market in confectionery: should they be in the distribution business? Even if some vertical integration looks useful, have they any of the requisite competence or experience for distribution? Or can they acquire these without damaging their core business? These questions and others about the nature of the business would have to be asked and answered affirmatively before worries about the ethics of the situation need to be addressed. As we said in chapter 1, ethics is not everything and everything is not ethics.

To take another example: the retailing business Little Home Stores (LHS) has a strategy of opening shops in prime high street sites. It is a healthy business buying into a depressed property market and used to landlords offering valuable inducements as part of long lease agreements. Sometimes shopfitting costs will be borne by the landlord; sometimes the rent clock will not start for two or three months; all of it accrues to the business's cash flow. Then LHS property department is offered a large sum of money not to take a property which they are in the process of acquiring. Although the offer comes through the landlord, LHS people believe that the source of the money is their main competitor, who clearly wants the site itself or, at least, does not want LHS to have it.

Before the discussion becomes bogged down in moral outrage on the ethics of bribery, it is worth asking the question about the nature of the business. Is LHS in retailing or property? If the answer is retailing, then property interests are there only to support this primary aim. When an action, such as giving up a prime site, undermines the central business aim, it should surely, at least in principle, be rejected.

Again, the point here is not to suggest that such issues are easily dealt with in the real, complex world but that bearing in mind primary questions on what *this* business is about can often help to clarify specific dilemmas. Ethics is not everything and everything is not ethics.

IMMORAL CAPITALISM?

What we have attempted so far is a brief analysis of the nature and aims of business where maximising owner value by trading for profit is identified as central to the activity. On this account, business is only possible within a capitalist system, that is, a system in which the market decides what is produced and in what quantities. As we have said, other forms of common activity (e.g. clubs) and other ways of providing goods and services (e.g. central planning) are possible but they are not businesses or business environments.

It is sometimes suggested that capitalism, with its market mechanism and profit motive, is an unethical system of production. Karl Marx was not the first but is probably the most famous exponent of this view. He argued that capitalism was exploitative; it made its profits by taking for itself the value that the workers added to basic commodities, giving in return only subsistence wages.[10] Even if the conditions within which people

[10] Karl Marx, *The Communist Manifesto*.

now work and the returns for which they work are rather different from Marx's late nineteenth-century experience, the argument remains as forceful as ever. Changes in working conditions, better wages and so on are merely, Marx would have said, tinkering with the system: they do not fundamentally change it. The immorality of the system is that it ties people into a method of production which treats them as only one of the factors of production. They may be paid a little more: their conditions may improve somewhat; but this does not change the system itself which, by its nature, must fail to treat them as human beings.

In his own terms, Marx is right. Capitalism, even in its people-oriented, late twentieth-century version, perceives its work-force as the 'human resource'. From a business point of view, its role is to produce as efficiently as possible in order to create the profit which is the aim of business.

And capitalist business is immoral precisely because it employs human beings in production and not in self-fulfilment and values them according to the market. But the market is not a system of morality or immorality, as Marx would have it. It is simply a mechanism. Nobody suggests that, because one individual is paid more than another, he or she is a better or more valuable human being. The market is not a means of identifying and giving to people what, on a moral or spiritual view, they deserve. The criteria are other than this, as they are in many fields of human activity. Sportsmen or opera singers do not get rewarded for being good people; university professors are supposed to be judged on their intellectual output, and warmth, humanity and even common decency are optional extras when promotions are under consideration.

Some people who become rich in a market system may be unpleasant, even immoral, people. But this does not make the system immoral, simply limited and partial: it does only what it is intended to do, which is to distribute according to contribution as seen by the market. This, as I shall say later, is the basis of distributive justice. Marx was, of course, not concerned with distributive justice, but with distribution according to need. It may often be a vague nostalgia for this idea that lies at the back of many criticisms of capitalism and induces some business people to respond by claiming for capitalism what they see as the moral high ground. Business is not immoral, they say; look how much good we do in society.

ETHICAL BUSINESS

But to take this line is to misconstrue what ethical activity in business is fundamentally about. It is not to be measured simply by the amount of a firm's corporate giving but is rather a matter of the proper conduct of day-to-day operations. The ethical organisation is one which pursues its aim of maximising long-term owner value. In setting itself up as a business, in accepting its shareholders' capital, in contracting its suppliers, in employing its people, it has created the expectation that it will act as a business. It would be the *failure* to aim to maximise returns for shareholders or to reward employees in proportion to their contribution to the enterprise which would be unethical.

Are there then no constraints on business's pursuit of its aim? Indeed there are, but they are not extraneous to business: they grow out of the nature of business itself. The ethical business will pursue long-term owner value, within the framework of distributive justice and the honesty and fair dealing without the presumption of which there could be no business. It is this framework which we will develop in detail in chapter 3.

CAN BUSINESSES BE MORAL AGENTS?

It is worth asking at this point in what way, if any, it makes sense to think of businesses as moral agents. Can a *business* really act in terms of distributive justice and common decency? It is often claimed, apparently with some justification, that it is individuals who make decisions; and it is individuals who carry them out. Not only does it make no logical sense to talk about *corporate* responsibility, but it is dangerous in that it erodes the sense of *individual* responsibility which is essential if business is to be ethically aware. To suggest that the company is the moral agent is to encourage the slide into personal irresponsibility – the 'I was only obeying orders' mentality.

However, in law, companies are often treated as the equivalent of moral agents, with corresponding rights and duties. In the

United States, in 1978, the Supreme Court granted corporations
the right to free speech, a right normally associated only with
individuals (*First National Bank of Boston* v. *Bellotti*). In Britain,
too, the Blue Arrow trial involved a charge of 'corporate fraud'
because, the prosecution claimed, it was individuals in their
corporate roles who were able to deceive the market in the ways
alleged and those involved would not have been able to do this
outside that corporate context.[11] This suggests that it is the
reputation of their companies as well as their personal good
name which allows people to be trusted and sometimes, therefore,
to misuse trust. Just as we can speak of corporations having
goals and interest, so we can speak of their having responsibilities
in the use of their power. If we cannot speak in such terms,
then we cannot judge corporations according to ethical standards.
But the question remains, what can it mean to say that ICI or
British Petroleum is responsible for a particular action?

Part of the answer must surely be that corporate decisions are
taken and implemented by individuals, but individuals acting in
their corporate capacity. Corporations, therefore, cannot simply
offload their responsibilities onto individuals; nor can individuals
abnegate responsibility in a business context. The trick is to get
the two to work together, which is largely a matter of company
values and culture and of the systems which operate within the
business. As we shall see, ensuring ethical operations is substan-
tially about ensuring that the systems and structures facilitate
and encourage them.

The establishment of proper structures and systems helps to
develop an ethical culture within the corporation by indicating
to all employees the attitudes and values of the company. If care
is clearly being taken both to analyse and to monitor company
decisions, there is less chance that a 'win at any price' attitude
will develop. People will tend to operate within the explicit,
and implicit, frameworks of the company culture and individual
managers are not left feeling that they operate in a moral vacuum,
into which they must import as much or as little of their personal
morality as their situation allows. In an organisation where
questions about outcomes and responsibilities are never raised,
the strategic decision to 'do it' may be read as implying 'and

[11] *Financial Times*, Court Report, 12 February 1991.

we don't care how'. This can hardly be the logic of the situation in a company which has set up structures precisely in order to monitor 'how'.

Such structures are particularly relevant in the case of very large companies, where the size and complexity of the organisation mean that decision and execution may be widely separated. Here all the problems of moral agency, of who exactly is responsible, become most acute. As one commentator has it, 'He who gives the order often cannot observe how it is carried out, and he who receives the order often cannot know exactly what was intended.'[12] Even in such circumstances businesses cannot deny responsibility for their intentional actions. Their size and complexity make it all the more imperative to have the structures within which decisions can be evaluated.

A NOTE ON THE STAKEHOLDER CONCEPT

The achievement of the aim of maximising value can quickly be seen as involving consideration of the interests of wider constituencies than simply shareholders. In this context, the idea of *stakeholders* is useful, reminding us as it does of the involvement of employees, customers, suppliers and the local and wider community in business's achievement of its aim. Such wider concerns do not dilute but reinforce the business aim. As is frequently argued, 'Concern for stakeholders and interest in profits are not mutually exclusive.'[13] Indeed, it is difficult to see how the one could be achieved without the other.

But the stakeholder framework cannot make business decisions for us and in some cases its terminology may be ambiguous or simplistic. As John Donaldson says, for example, the 'public good' is often, at best, elusive.[14] And, in similar vein, Sir Adrian Cadbury asks, 'Who are the employees?'[15] Again, it should not be thought that ethical decisions in business are simply a matter of deciding between the competing claims of the various stake-

---

[12] James Q. Wilson, Adam Smith on business ethics, *California Management Review*, vol. 32, no. 1, 1989, p. 68.
[13] K. Davis, Five propositions for social responsibility, *Business Horizons*, vol. 18, no. 3, 1975, p. 19.
[14] J. Donaldson, *Key issues in Business Ethics*, Academic Press, 1989, p. 123.
[15] A. Cadbury; *The Company Chairman*, Director Books, 1990, p. 151.

holders. Yet the stakeholder notion identifies an important set of relationships. In pursuing its aim, within the context of distributive justice and common decency, the business must decide how it will treat its shareholders, employees, customers and so on. Conversely, it is worth asking how the various stakeholders should relate to businesses. What, for example, are the responsibilities of employees – or shareholders? These too are issues I will raise when I come to investigate specific ethical concerns in part II of the book.

By defining business in terms of its aim and relating the achievement of that aim to the ethical imperatives inherent in business itself and not extraneous to it, I have tried to show that business ethics is firmly embedded in the business decision-making process. Business ethics is not an occasionally interesting but ultimately academic discussion about how good or bad business should be. Nor is it intent on simply moralising, on revealing the pathologies of the modern corporation and suggesting how these can be redeemed through good works. Still less is it the demand that business solve all our social problems, from environmental pollution to illiteracy and discrimination. Its claim is more modest and more realistic than any of these: it is to offer a framework within which business dilemmas can be systematically addressed. It is not a panacea but a complex exercise in practical ethics.

3

The ethical decision model

> Will not the knowledge of [the good], then, have a great
> influence on life? Shall we not, like archers who have a mark
> to aim at, be more likely to hit upon what is right?
>
> (Aristotle, *The Nicomachean Ethics*)

Before we can identify the principles and set the framework
within which business ethics can proceed, we need to be clear
not only about the nature of business but about the nature of
ethics. We have already raised some of the arguments in general
terms in chapter 1, about what business ethics is and is not and
why we need it. This is worth reiterating now, along with the
argument about the nature and aim of business (chapter 2), so
that, putting these together with a more specific account of the
nature of ethics itself, we may set the context within which an
ethical decision model (EDM) can be developed. The EDM is not
a formula, the terms of which can be substituted with numerical
precision. As we shall see, it is rather a series of questions which
aim to eliminate the irrelevant information, identify the ethical
problem (if there is one) and suggest the principles on which an
ethical solution may be based.

WHY BUSINESS ETHICS IS NECESSARY

Business ethics is, as I have said, not an enquiry into the foun-
dations of ethics in general or into the justifications for competing
moral philosophies. It takes for granted the existence of ethics, as
it takes the existence of business as given. Furthermore, not all
business decisions are ethical ones. How to organise your plant,
what corporate logo to choose or which hurdle rate to apply are
not ethical dilemmas. Business ethics starts with specific and
identifiable moral dilemmas which emerge in the course of business

42

activity and is concerned not to moralise but to offer a framework for the logical analysis of such dilemmas. It is a branch of practical ethics, the role of which is to help business people think more clearly about moral problems which face them from day to day in business. It does this, to begin with, by making *explicit* the often implicit aspirations, aims and values of business, and of *this* particular business. Business ethics, seen in this way, is simply a tool, like management accounts or, say, the Capital Asset Pricing Model, to help structure the thinking through of what can be complex, messy, multi-dimensional problems; and to help eliminate the 'noise' of irrelevant information and detail. It aims to suggest *how*, not *what*, to think about moral matters. And it starts from the business aim.

Moreover, it is an essential part of business decision-making. Accounting structures, financial theories, econometric models, all aim to be explanatory frameworks which aspire to give greater control over business decisions, but all are limited to certain areas of the business. Business ethics has similarities to such theories but is wider in its applications in seeking to identify and take account of the multi-dimensional relationships of business practice. Ethical positions are unavoidable in business, where decisions are taken all the time which involve sifting values and weighing up priorities. If we are not just to be *ad hoc* or arbitrary, we need a structure for decision-taking and we need to have thought through some basic questions about the nature of business in general, the aims of *this* business and the relations between the sometimes competing claims of groups of people involved with the business.

WHAT ARE THE PRINCIPLES OF BUSINESS ETHICS?

Now that we have established the parameters and purpose of business ethics, we can begin to identify its main principles. But, before we do this, it is important to establish that business ethics is not a special kind of ethics, an ethics of a lower order than 'ordinary' morality. There is no such thing as a separate business ethic or a set of principles specific only to the conduct of business. Ethics is concerned with the principles of good and evil, which are universal and eternal. It may well be that, as science and technology develop, for example, we become preoccupied by one quandary rather than another, but the ethical *principles* remain the same.

Again, although ethics may take as its focus the areas of medicine or sport or science as well as business, it is the typical problems and not the principles of ethics which are area-specific. There is no special code of *business* ethics; rather there are questions and dilemmas, about remuneration, whistle-blowing, product safety and so on, which arise mainly in the course of business activity but which can be dealt with in terms of universal moral principles. And there are many values which we intuitively recognise as such. Honesty, reliability, just and fair dealing are universally recognised as right, just as lying, cheating, stealing, cowardice and irresponsibility are recognised as wrong. Breaking agreements, treating people shabbily, telling lies, taking more than your due are wrong – in business as in any other aspect of life.

This is not to say that it is always easy to determine exactly how a certain activity is properly described (what exactly counts as honest or fair in this situation, for example?) and difficult choices may sometimes have to be made between values. Principles are not always easily reconcilable; it is not hard to decide between the blacks and whites, but much more difficult to determine the right course among the shades of grey. In spite of the difficulties, however, business ethics attempts to apply general moral principles to business activities in order to resolve, or at least clarify, the moral issues which typically arise in business.

Relativism and subjectivism

The first issue is concerned with whether 'moral principles' of which we are speaking are not essentially relativistic or even subjective. It is rather unfashionable in our pluralist society to declare for anything as apparently undemocratic as moral absolutes. Aren't everybody's moral views as good as everybody else's? Whose values or principles are we really talking about here – those of Christianity or Judaism or Islam or the government of the day or the European Community or the Confederation of British Industry or, indeed, the Chairman of the Board? Yet surely not all moral codes have equal value. Some principles just do make better sense of the moral universe than others and certainly some are more consistently relevant in the context of business. We want businesses to be honest and fair with their stakeholders; we do not want them to ignore the interests of the wider community or pollute the environment. We must assume these objectives to be statements of principle and not merely *expressions of taste*. If they are not principles, we are left in the no-man's-land of relativism: you prefer justice and fairness while I prefer chicanery and dishonesty, just as you may prefer cream in your coffee while I like it black. Personal taste can be no basis for moral argument.

The importance of moral principles is that they allow us to identify the essential and unvarying features of differing situations and then to apply them in dealing with real-life problems. In business ethics, principles give us a set of criteria in terms of which to judge acceptable business practice, criteria which can be applied consistently over time and place, argued for and applied to real-life situations. Such principles are not really so hard to identify although they may be harder to apply. There is little disagreement over widely different creeds and cultures about basic moral values. There is no society in which lying and cheating are seen as good or where honesty and decency are condemned.

Some moral principles will be particularly relevant to business dealings and it is these which we should now try to identify. They are principles which emerge from the nature and aim of business itself and without which business may not be true to that nature or achieve that end.

Common decency

Although the more spectacular and public examples of unethical behaviour in business – insider trading or various kinds of corporate tragedy[1] – are the issues which grab the headlines, it is in the normal, everyday activities of the business that ethical principles need most to be applied. It is largely in how people treat other people within the company, the boss, the secretary, the

---

[1] 'Corporate tragedy' refers to all disasters which befall businesses – from an explosion in a plant to an aeroplane crash – in which employees, customers or members of the public are killed, injured or otherwise put at risk.

salesperson the retailer and so on, that the ethical climate of the business is set. Without this awareness of personal relationships, the moral context of the business is lost and the grosser forms of unethical behaviour can emerge almost unchallenged. Because of this, one of the basic principles of business ethics is simply that of *common decency*: that is, the maintenance of standards of ordinary decent behaviour by all to all associated with the business. And all includes not only employees at every level but all stakeholders. It is as important to be honest with your suppliers as it is with your shareholders and to be as decent with your customers as you are with your employees.

Common decency does not mean being nice to people or being altruistic but treating people in a way which allows their legitimate expectations to be met, so liberating them to pursue their roles in the business in the secure knowledge that their contribution will be recognised and their expectations fulfilled. Decency means honest and responsible treatment of those with whom one comes in contact and this emerges as a principle from the identified aim of the business itself. If stakeholders cannot see that they will be dealt with honestly and in a responsible manner, there is little reason why they should commit themselves to the success of the business.

Justice

The other fundamental value of business ethics, again emerging from the aim of business itself, is *justice* in the distribution of rewards, privileges and responsibilities. Distributive justice relates rewards to contribution so that, as far as possible, those who contribute most to the business and the fulfilment of its aim will be rewarded proportionately more than those who contribute less. An enterprise which does not reward in this way, and so encourage those who contribute to its aim, is selfdefeating. The purpose of a business is to achieve long-term owner value, and pay and promotions should reflect contribution to this, just as such rewards should go in the universities to those who make the greatest academic contribution, or in an orchestra to those who make the greatest musical contribution.

If distributive justice is not the criterion here, if promotions in a business were to be based on who was the best friend or nearest relation of the chief executive, who was the kindest or most humane employee or who could play the piano best, the aim of the business would not be served. Justice, like decency, is central to the achievement of long-term owner value and, in this sense, emerges from the very notion of business itself.

Other ethical principles may be relevant in particular business contexts: it is possible to imagine scenarios in which the traditional deadly sins of pride, covetousness, lust, anger, gluttony, envy and sloth could relate to business practice. It is perhaps less easy but still possible to construct a place for the traditional virtues like humility, chastity, meekness and temperance. They are normally, however, irrelevant or supererogatory in a business context. In general, the ethical case will be served by the principles of decency (which includes honesty, responsibility and reliability) and justice (which includes fairness). These values will be the ones we consistently refer to in analysing business ethics problems. They may have slightly different emphases in different contexts but they are generally applicable in all business situations.

THE ETHICAL DECISION MODEL (EDM)

We have now set the framework within which specific problems in business ethics can be analysed. We have identified the nature both of business and of ethics and shown that ethics is not identical with law or religion but that the expectation must be that the business will act within the law. Similarly, ethics does not necessarily entail suffering or altruism; and something which is beneficial to the business can also be ethical.

Again, we have established that motives and behaviour can be separated; in order to do the right thing, which is what the ethical business must be about, businesses do not have to be motivated exclusively by ethical considerations. Mixed motives are normal and acceptable.

Given this background, we are now in a position to develop a model or framework within which business ethics problems can be analysed or assessed. Such a framework, which I call the ethical decision model (EDM) is not a formula but rather a series of questions which can be used to clarify the nature of particular problems and how, if possible, they can be solved.

The framework draws our attention to the relevant issues and offers a way forward which does not deny the purpose of the enterprise itself.

1. What is the question? (What is really at stake? Who is affected? How?)
2. How does it affect *this* business?
3. What are the external constraints (legal, regulatory, market etc.)?
4. Apply the ethical principles. (Which of the various options conform to justice and decency while maintaining long-term owner value?)

1. What is the question?

The first thing to do when confronted with an apparent ethical issue is to be clear exactly what the question is, for *this business, now*. Businesses are not required to solve the world's general moral problems and taking a question in the abstract is unlikely to be helpful in dealing with the limited, specific situation for which action is needed now. Many questions, posed in the abstract, turn out, on analysis, to be confusing or meaningless. For example, 'Are hostile takeovers a good thing?' may seem to pose a real problem in business ethics but, as it stands, it is so general as to be virtually unanswerable. It might be raising questions of public policy, economic theory, financial management or power politics as well as business ethics. Good for what, we might ask? For redistributing assets, building up a business empire, attracting new shareholders? And good for whom? For the predator, the shareholder, the board, the business's bankers, the government, the Treasury or even the country as a whole?

Luckily, a particular business will normally be addressing this kind of question in a quite specific context in which the first step is simply to analyse the question, to find out what precisely is at stake and who will be affected, what kind of action might be required, over what period and on whose responsibility. It is only by answering those and related questions that the issue itself will become clear.

2. Is it relevant to this business?

It may emerge from the above analysis that the question is not relevant to this business and so there is no business ethics issue for the business to resolve. It is not the role of business to philosophise about abstract ethical issues and, although it may be interesting to discuss such ideas, it will probably not contribute to long-term owner value. A one-man business will not have to spend time pondering a detailed remuneration policy any more than a corner sweet shop will need to work out its position on bribery world-wide.

3. What are the external constraints on the business?

A question may also turn out not to be relevant for a particular business because it is constrained in some way, for example by the law or the market. If some particular course of action is against a law or regulation, there is normally no need to agonise over the ethical dimension at all. For example, foreign ownership constraints apply in some countries so that only a minority holding by an alien is possible; concern about the morality of a hostile takeover would be, in such circumstances, beside the point. Again, if the cost of mounting a takeover were prohibitive or if the application of even the lowest hurdle rate could not show a profit, the business decision is, in effect, taken without recourse to any ethical considerations. Ethics is not everything and everything is not ethics.

4. Apply the ethical principles.

If, after such an analysis, it emerges that there is indeed an ethical issue for this business to face at this time, the principles outlined above need to be applied and the implications of justice and decency for the business's aim worked out. Proposed actions need to be looked at in terms of the fundamental objective of all business – establishing long-term owner value. This both eliminates some questions and points to the answer to others. Should a business make charitable contributions? Should it support the arts? Should it sponsor enterprise in the local community? Posed thus, the answer is always no. The aim of the business is neither charitable nor artistic. Yet to the extent that such activities do contribute to the business aim and can be shown to do so (or their opposites shown to detract from it) they should be pursued. What concern should the business have for its employees' welfare or its suppliers' interests? Common decency and justice may seem expensive but the failure to honour them may be far more so.

It may not always be easy to assess shareholder value; valuable contributions may well be indirect and long-term; quantification may be difficult. But it is also difficult to quantify many other factors in business, the value of which are routinely taken for granted. For information technology, for example, it is often much easier to determine costs than to quantify benefits.

The most serious problems arise for business in this area when the *obligation* which business has to create shareholder value is not appreciated either by those inside the business or by those outside. If those inside the business lose sight of the business aim, they may engage in activities which undermine that aim and so jeopardise the business. If those outside the business see the business as other than it is, as a source of funds for their own enterprise or activity, for example, they may believe the business's refusal to become involved in some worthwhile but non-business goal is 'immoral'. But in pursuing its aim the business is doing exactly what it ought to do and it is those who expect it to be seeking other than long-term owner value who are confused.

Again, this is not to say that business should not be ethical – generous to its employees and careful of the environment. But ultimately, management's responsibility within the business is to be profitable, not to be kind, although as I have said more than once, common decency tends to fall through to the bottom line.

But what counts as ethical or unethical action in the business context? Isn't business a 'dog-eat-dog' affair where people cannot afford to be too scrupulous? Isn't this the real problem for business ethics, that many business activities by their very nature encourage immorality? Employees are not decently treated because it is too expensive to do so; advertising is inherently misleading because it has to grow the market regardless; successful salesmen cannot be entirely honest. We will deal with these and other issues in more detail in subsequent chapters but for the moment, let us look briefly at the question of honesty in business. The problem is not posed in any very sophisticated way by the Oxford Street trader mentioned in chapter 1 who offers 'solid gold' bracelets for £10. Here one might say that most people would know what they were buying in such circumstances and that the lies are so patent and obvious that they can scarcely aim seriously to deceive. But what about the half-truths typical of some sales techniques or the failure to mention other relevant factors: that the 'des. res.' is built over an old mine shaft, or that, although the capital outlay is modest, the running costs are astronomical?

In such situations, it is worth remembering the notion of *appropriateness*. 'The truth, the whole truth and nothing but the truth' strictly applied is probably only appropriate in a court of law. Salespeople are not the only ones who modify their responses to the expectations of others in the circumstances. A polite greeting which enquires how you are is not really intended to elicit a detailed account of the state of your health and most people respond not, as they would see it, evasively but appropriately in the circumstances. Similarly, most people of average politeness and social skill would not necessarily tell the whole truth and nothing but if a friend asked their opinion of a new outfit or, worse, a new baby. Similarly, salespeople operate within a social context where certain expectations are set: they are there, and understood to be there, to sell, not to give general consumer information. They will, if they have plans to be in business long term, tell the truth but it may not be the whole truth and nothing but; it should, however, not seek to deceive and should be appropriate in the circumstances.

Rather than being unrealistic, honesty in business dealings carries, in general, a high premium. It is not simply 'Pollyannaish' to claim that this principle is central to sustained business success because maximising value long term requires the continuing belief by all stakeholders that the business will act with honesty, responsibility and reliability – that is, with common decency. Common decency contributes to long-term owner value, as we have shown, by giving those who work for the business the security to perform their functions without endlessly protecting their backs. People know where they stand, will not be encouraged to have unrealistic expectations of the business, nor will their realistic expectations be disappointed. Again and again we will see the importance of good communications – both internally and externally – in the successful and the ethical business. Rumour and uncertainty are counter-productive; they take people's minds off the job and create an atmosphere of uncertainty and mistrust. Even if it is to admit to no definitive answers or to give bad news, it is essential that management communicate its thinking. Examples abound of problems being hugely exacerbated for a business by lack of communication and, on the other hand, of the effects on both morale and share price of the honest acknowledgement of a problem.

Much of the rest of this book will look at a variety of common business ethics problems which, for convenience of exposition and reference, have been gathered under functional heads. In the real business world, of course, such issues are much less neat and tidy.

PART II

The ethical questions

4

Human resources

> In business . . . the role of ethics is to apply general ethical
> values and principles not *to* particular situations but *in* par-
> ticular situations.
>
> (Jack Mahoney)

> The ideal company would not need a human resource
> activity, just as an ideal world would not require doctors.
>
> (Robert Ayling, Human Resources Director,
British Airways)

In the nineteenth century, they were the 'workers'. Later, the
class associations of that term made it incompatible with the
claims of modern democracy and they became 'staff'. Then, in
the terms of scientific management, they were 'personnel' before
finally being transformed into 'human resources'.[1] Thus does our
changing language neatly convey the different emphases which
we have laid at different times on the role and status of employees.
Not that all nineteenth-century employers were unsympathetic
to their workers' interests – one has only to think of the Rowntrees
or Cadburys or of Leverhulme at Port Sunlight to dismiss that
idea – but 'workers' they were and remained, engendering a
largely paternalistic concern for their well-being. The safe but
impersonal 'staff' emphasised differentiation and hierarchy, while
'personnel' suggested that the problem of people had been managed once for all within a bureaucratic structure of hiring and
firing arrangements and management/union negotiation. The
human resource concept, which became popular in the 1980s,
puts employees at the centre of the business stage. Companies
which use their human resources effectively, it is claimed, gain
a competitive advantage as employees are more committed and

---

[1] See, An idea whose time has come, *The Financial Times*, 28 January 1991, p. 11.

productive if they are well-informed, and have a sense of their own autonomy.

What does this mean for the ethical enterprise? What should be the attitude of business to its employees? As we have already argued, the aim is and must be the business one of the creation of long-term owner value. We have also argued that this is most likely to be achieved if affairs are clearly conducted with decency and fairness. As it stands, however, this is a rather abstract argument and says nothing about how such aims might be translated into policy on recruitment, remuneration, training or redundancy. What this chapter, and the following 'functional' ones, will attempt to do is apply these principles within the business.

A word of caution is perhaps in order at the start: this book is not a manual or a rule-book which can simply be looked up, digested and applied direct to particular situations. There is always an important element of judgement involved in any business decision and only those directly involved will be in a position finally to make that judgement in any particular case. Business people, in other words, know their own businesses best. There is no suggestion that the framework offered here can simply be taken over and slavishly applied to a particular business. However, as we have emphasised in part I, it is important to begin by asking the right questions; to refrain from addressing ethical issues in the abstract; to identify limited and specific questions as they affect *this* business; and to apply the standards of decency and distributive justice which contribute to the business aim. As Jack Mahoney so rightly says,

> It is of the true nature of all applied ethics that it should begin within actual problematic situations, and not simply address them from the outside by prescribing prepackaged answers. In business . . . the role of ethics is to apply general ethical values and principles not *to* particular situations but *in* particular situations.[2]

The point is well made. What is on offer here, then, is not a spurious generalised solution to all ethical dilemmas in business but a framework which, in putting the right questions, will elicit, in the particular case, the right answers.

---

[2] J. Mahoney, *Teaching Business Ethics in the UK, Europe and the USA: A Comparative Study*, Athlone, 1991, pp. 169–70.

BUSINESS AND EMPLOYEE

I have already discussed at some length what the aim of business is: the production of long-term shareholder value. Business does not exist, then, primarily to improve the quality of life of employees. Even a commentator as committed to the social role of business as Charles Handy is clear that 'it is the organisation's job to deliver; it is not its job to be everyone's alternative community, providing meaning and work for all for life'.[3] But, as we have also already indicated, the achievement of this primary aim involves some crucial strategic action in relation to the business's stakeholders. In this context, employees must be accounted as central stakeholders in the business, as a group whose needs within the business must be met if the business itself is to prosper. Relationships of decency and trust within a business are not, therefore, just an optional extra but are central to the achievement of the business aim. Employees who encounter bad conditions of work – whether in the form of dirty lavatories, lack of privacy or unjust wage structures, will be unwilling to make any great efforts for the business. They may, through force of circumstances, personal or economic, stay with the business but they can hardly be expected to give of their best. They will do unto the business as it has done unto them. As one CEO graphically puts it:

Do you really imagine that an individual after being told explicitly and by long example that his company has no responsibility to him or to any one else except insofar as it maximises its legal profits . . . will be of a mind to make a loyal commitment to the welfare and progress of his company . . . Or do you imagine that such a worker . . . might be inclined to maximise his own legal profits by stretching out the work so that he can get more overtime – or perhaps even a little Sunday double time?[4]

And just as employees need to believe in the company's commitment to treating them with decency, so they need to believe that they will be treated justly and fairly, that they will not be used and then arbitrarily rejected. As celebrated a wheeler-dealer as Richard Branson is convinced that the latter behaviour is essen-

---

[3] C. Handy, *The Age of Unreason*, Century Hutcheson, 1989.
[4] J. Irwin Miller, CEO, Cummins Engine Company, quoted in R. Solomon and K. Hanson, *It's Good Business*, Atheneum, 1985, p. 194.

tially self-defeating. While recognising that the stereotype of the
successful entrepreneur is someone who tramples all over everybody to get what he wants, Branson begs to differ: 'if you can
srike a fair deal with people they'll come back for more. In the
long run, your business will do that much better', and he goes
on, 'Staff are the most important asset . . . our philosophy [of
employee care] means that the shareholders actually benefit in
the long run.'[5]

IS HUMAN RESOURCE MANAGEMENT EFFECTIVE AND/OR MANIPULATIVE?

This view of human resource management is very seductive and
fits well with our framework of the business aim pursued in the
context of stakeholder requirements. There are, however, at least
two general questions which need to be raised before we go on
to look at the specifics of employee relations. The first is whether,
in courting their employees, businesses will really gain in productivity. This is largely an empirical question but so far little
research has been done to resolve it one way or another. There
is, as we have said, a good theoretical case, backed up by the
anecdotal evidence of many business people, that if employees
are treated decently and in conformity with distributive justice,
they will perform better.

Some recent research on a limited aspect of human resource
management, however, seems to cast doubt on its value as a
way of gaining workers' trust, encouraging harder work and
so enhancing productivity. In a research report on employee
involvement schemes in the American metal-working sector, it
was found that where joint management/shopfloor problem-
solving committees were operating, in many cases productivity
(as measured by total production time per unit of output) actually
fell.[6] This is not, of course, an indictment of the whole process
of worker consultation; the firms involved may have been inefficient for reasons quite other than their employee involvement

---

[5] Quoted in *Management Week*, July 1991, p. 50.
[6] *Technology Review*, Massachusetts Institute of Technology, January 1991, p. 74. Quoted by Michael Dixon in the *Financial Times*, 20 February 1991, p. 15.

policies, or their particular consultation processes may have been defective in crucial respects.

At this stage, however, it is worth pointing out that, although more detailed empirical work needs to be done on many aspects of human resource management, the theory of employee involvement, care and concern seems sound and is certainly more in tune with today's social attitudes than a more hierarchical or *dirigiste* form of management. It is what employees have come to expect of better companies and this alone makes it more likely to help in achieving the business aim.

The other question which should not be ducked at this stage is how far company provision for employees should go. It may be ethically impeccable to take care of employees' health, training, pensions, even redundancy investment, but what about counselling services for employees who are divorcing or trying to adopt children or find care for elderly relatives? Such services are indeed provided by some American companies such as Hewlett-Packard and IBM, who argue that they prevent resignations and absenteeism among workers with difficult family circumstances and thereby avoid rehiring and retraining costs.[7] Is this ethical involvement, based on the desire to make sure that staff are not distracted from their work by worry about domestic problems, or is it an unacceptable paternalism? Is it indicative of a proper care and concern for the workforce or does it show a sinister desire on the part of businesses to manipulate their staff and tie them into a company which knows too much about them and on which they may become dependent for a great deal more than their wage-packet?

The answers to these questions are not straightforward but the model I have suggested, based on the business's aim, is clearly helpful. Again, as I have said, such questions cannot be answered in the abstract (although they are nearly always posed thus). The acceptability and usefulness of such policies within a business will largely depend on the business itself, on its specific aims and on its culture and traditions. Many highly successful companies have always taken a very paternalistic line with employees – one thinks immediately of Marks and Spencer or IBM. On the other hand, the same level of concern suddenly

[7] See *The Times*, 28 August 1991, p. 12.

visited on the employees of a small software development business would almost certainly be seen as manipulative – and would therefore be counter-productive.

The most important consideration here is whether the services or supports offered to employees are productive of the business aim. They should not be offered as a substitute for the role of state or family or church or because human resource managers have some grandiose notion that they are in business to save the world. They may, however, appropriately be offered if the judgement is made that their provision will help people to do their jobs more effectively. The need to make a judgement does not go away but the identification of the correct criteria at least makes it possible to come to the correct conclusion.

WHAT THE EMPLOYEE OWES TO THE BUSINESS

So far, we have been setting the framework within which we can review the various aspects of human resource management – recruitment, remuneration and so on – by looking at how the business should relate to its employees. We have suggested that common decency and distributive justice take us a long way in achieving the business aim. If these then become the basis of what the business owes its employees, what do the employees owe the business?

There is no doubt that the most valuable and productive employees are those who give their loyalty to the business. It is expensive to train people and if they immediately move on, feeling no loyalty, the loss to the business is clear and unequivocal. If information is shared with employees, on the basis that an open atmosphere is the most productive working environment, and they then walk off to a competitor, the loss is again real and hard. The hope is that people who are treated decently will reciprocate by being decent in return. And so the circle is completed: a business which gets loyalty from its staff will reinforce its own policies of fairness and so on.

Of course, such actions have to start somewhere and it is in the decisions of the business *vis-à-vis* employees that ethical attitudes are bred. But for the process to aid the business aim, well-treated employees must also treat the business well. This element of reciprocity is inherent in most ethical action and is always worth bearing in mind in the context of business activity. Businesses have responsibilities to their stakeholders – including employees – and their stakeholders have responsibilities towards them.

RECRUITMENT

What should be the criteria in terms of which the ethical organisation recruits? Again, fundamental here must be the business purpose of enhancing long-term shareholder value. 'Recruiters are in the business of risk minimisation', says Mike Lymath of HMV.[8] And he goes on to explain that this is not just the minimising of risk for the organisation of the costs of recruitment and training but of the risk to existing employees if the wrong person is recruited and the risk to the new employee if s/he is disgruntled and unsuitable. The recruiter, then, is there to meet the needs of the organisation and the needs of the individual; they are, in effect, two sides of the same coin. So what are the processes by which this synthesis is achieved? Obviously, recruiters must be very clear about the nature of the job to be done; they must then identify the abilities necessary to do that job, to meet the performance standards required. It is in the context of measurement and assessment of performance that problems arise.

It is sometimes argued, for example, that to recruit simply on the basis of credentials – degrees or professional qualifications – is unfair. It may exclude from consideration some people who could have done the job but simply do not have the formal qualification demanded. Unless the qualification is essential to the carrying out of the duties required, it is argued that it may just narrow the field unnecessarily and unfairly. While it may be quite reasonable to insist on recruiting a lawyer to look after your commercial contracts, do you really need a graduate or an accountant in customer relations? It will, of course, depend on the job but the predisposition to look for *objective* as opposed to *credential* criteria may be to the advantage of the business, first in making those responsible identify very clearly the nature and requirements of the job and also in increasing the numbers of

[8] Interview with Mike Lymath, Human Resource Director, HMV Group Ltd.

those who can apply to include not only the formally qualified but also the less qualified who are nevertheless able and experienced.

If this route is chosen, the question then becomes one of measuring applicants' ability to meet the required performance standards of the job. The business needs to learn about people in order to make the necessary judgements, to minimise risk to the business and to the individual (who can have no desire to end up in the wrong job). But how much has the business a right to know and what are legitimate ways of finding out?

The business has a duty in recruiting to fit the job to the appropriate person and in so doing it will legitimately seek information about job candidates. Job interviews, assessments and tests, however, are not simply one-way. They not only tell the business about the candidate, they also tell the candidate about the business. Tests of dubious validity or involving lack of respect for privacy will be harmful to the business. They may make a suitable candidate reflect on whether s/he really wants to work for an organisation which operates in such a way. It is important that the ethical business adopts recruitment criteria which achieve the business end of acquiring relevant knowledge about the candidate without undermining the business end by putting off the most suitable people.

The main criteria here should be:

RELEVANCE of the information sought and of any tests used;

OPENNESS in what the tests are designed to show;

SOUNDNESS of the tests and their results;

RESPECT for the privacy of the individual.

It should also be added that such tests should be seen as supporting information only and not used in isolation.

If we apply these criteria to the various forms of testing used by businesses in recruiting their staff, we can begin to make some distinctions between them. Critical reasoning tests, for example, are often employed to determine both numerical and verbal skills. Such skills are clearly relevant for a great many jobs and the tests themselves show, in the view of most businesses, a successful record. They are used openly and do not impinge on the privacy of candidates and are therefore an acceptable way of acquiring recruitment information.

Psychometric tests (i.e. psychological testing of one kind or another) are increasingly used by recruiters. Here, once the qualities needed for a certain job have been specified, tests claim to be able to identify which candidates have such qualities. If the relevance of the information obtained by such testing is accepted, the soundness of the results may still be questionable. Although most companies who use such tests agree that they are not directly predictive, nor are they useful on their own, many claim that they are a legitimate aid to successful recruitment. The British Psychological Society validates the occupational use of tests and testers and has produced guidelines on the use of tests and a code of good practice.

A study carried out for a brewing firm, for example, identified certain qualities which, it was claimed, were common to successful pub managers. They included better verbal reasoning than the average, a higher degree of numeracy, greater assertiveness, enjoyment in working with people and greater conscientiousness. The brewing company was predictably unimpressed with this rather obvious list but when they began to use the tests for such qualities in their recruitment of pub managers, they claimed to have cut their failure rates by half.[9]

If the tests themselves are relevant and open, then, does it matter whether or not their methodology is entirely clear? The proof of the pudding, one might say, is in the eating and if they produce results, they are legitimate. The problem with this position is that, as it stands, it leaves the way open for any number of unsubstantiated claims in the area. Personality testing, even if we are not entirely clear about how it works, is impeccably scientific by comparison with clairvoyance, for example. And lest it be thought that this is too fanciful an example, there is at least one extra-sensory perception consultant working in Britain.[10] And the President of the Astrological Association has been quoted as claiming an increase in the number of companies asking for astrological charts which indicate the likely performance of job applicants.[11]

Whether these tests or predictions 'work' or not is a matter for the businesses involved to decide. Only they can judge whether they think their use minimises the risk of recruiting the

[9] Quoted in *In Business*, Radio 4, 21 April 1991.
[10] Business advice is all in the mind, *The Financial Times*, 16 July 1991, p. 11.
[11] Business advice.

wrong person (or maximises the chance of getting the right person). This is not the place to go into the likelihood of what seems like good and objective advice simply reinforcing the preconceptions and prejudices of the recipient (which is obviously a problem with all consultancy). But for the ethical organisation, there are perhaps other considerations to take into account. What, for example, is the message given to employees or potential employees if recruitment decisions are seen to be taken, even partly, on the basis of unproved tests? Is there something dangerously arbitrary about the fact that people can be instated (and perhaps removed?) as a result of their outcomes? The ethos of suspicion and uncertainty that this might engender could well deter suitable people and would almost certainly undermine belief in the decency and fairness of the business. This kind of argument is most telling against polygraphic testing (the lie detector). The use of polygraphs is now illegal in the USA but both there and in Britain new psychometric tests have been devised which claim to show the honesty/integrity of job applicants. Is this kind of test, the so-called 'son of polygraph', more acceptable than its parent, which was seen as violating the privacy of applicants?

Those who use such tests – often in the retailing and banking sectors where employees may be required to handle money or valuable merchandise – would claim that the relevance of this information is obvious, that they are open in their use of the tests and that the tests themselves have a proven record of accuracy. However, the openness may be in question when the questions asked are not overtly related to honesty or integrity (examples include: How restless are you? How often do you smile? How many people do you like?). Equally, the soundness of the tests is certainly not proven. The American Psychological Society found that honesty/integrity tests were accurate in three out of four cases, which compares favourably with other forms of testing commonly used (e.g. educational tests). However, the Office of Technology Assessment of the United States Congress, having looked at this research, said that it could not, as currently presented, validate the tests.[12]

In addition to worries about the soundness of such tests, there must be concern about the possible violation of privacy involved.

---

[12] Business advice.

They are intrusive and they do ask questions whose bearing on the job applied for may be less than immediately relevant. All of this should give businesses pause and have them ask whether the benefits they believe they derive from the use of such testing are outweighed by the uncertainty of the tests themselves and the possible loss of privacy to employees. And at the back of this whole issue is the question of what message such tests convey to employees themselves. As one Human Resource Director (in a retailing organisation) said, 'You're telling the world and the employees the values of your organisation: if you suggest "we think you're all at it" [i.e. stealing] you engender a climate where they may think they might as well be.'[13] One is reminded of the chain store which issued its sales assistants with pocketless overalls. After that, there was no need to talk explicitly about a lack of trust in the business.

EQUALITY IN THE WORKPLACE

At the stages of both recruitment and promotion, questions may arise about opportunities for women, ethnic minorities, older and handicapped workers. Taking the business aim as paramount, the ground rules have already been set in the discussion on recruitment. The aim of the recruiter must be to identify the best person for the job (or, more likely, to give line managers a shortlist of people who could perform well). This will involve acquiring the relevant information about the candidates' abilities, qualifications and experience. Being black or female or over fifty will, in most cases, be neither here nor there. It is possible, of course, to think of circumstances when such factors may be not only relevant but central: a black actor required for a television commercial or a female attendant for a ladies' lavatory. In general, however, skin colour and sex are not job-relevant and the business will pursue its aim most successfully if it concentrates on getting the best person for the job.

In the past and sometimes still, businesses were loath to employ women because they believed that they would get married and have children and so lose the business its investment in training and development. As more women are continuing to work after

---

[13] Mike Lymath interview.

marriage, taking only short career breaks to have children, and
the birthrate itself has fallen, employers are having to rethink
their assumption that female staff are a business risk. Without
going into the contentious area of whether female management
styles are more suited to today's teamworking and collective
decision-taking, there are several reasons why the recruitment of
women can be seen as contributing to business success.

To begin with, women now make up around half of all university undergraduates. Women are a significant percentage of the
pool of talent for which employers are fighting and they can no
longer afford to favour men at the risk of losing in the fight to
attract the best and the brightest. As Mike Heron, who was
Director of Personnel at Unilever says, 'We need as much talent
as we can get.' Organisations have to seek women out, he
continues, if only because, 'if you take the other route, then
you've got to have twice your share of the talented men. In a
market economy, that's going to cost a lot of money.'[14]

In addition, organisations employing a good proportion of
women will be perceived as having caught the *Zeitgeist* and be
viewed as progressive and responsible. This will undoubtedly
make them more attractive to future employees, both women
and men, and probably also to customers and shareholders.

But what if some of those within the business do not see
themselves as progressive? What if they are happy to retain their
sexist or racist attitudes? What should happen, for example, if
the recruitment system identifies the best person for the job as
a woman but the job involves being part of a small team which
is self-consciously male chauvinist? They may tell sexist jokes
but their morale is very high, they get on with each other
extremely well and their productivity is second to none. Is the
decision to give the job to the female applicant the right one?
Going back to the framework developed in chapter 3, what is
the question at issue here? To begin with, it is not the *abstract*
one about the rights of women employees (the interests of the
particular woman involved here are, of course, clearly an issue).
Rather, it is a question about how the ends of the business are
to be achieved in an ethical way. This may seem to lead inevitably
to the conclusion that, if the woman's presence will be disruptive

---

[14] Quoted in *No room for new faces at the top*, *The Financial Times*, 7 May 1991, p. 14.

to the group, which will consequently not perform so well, the decision is already made; the woman, however able, is not the most suitable candidate for the job. Her appointment will not achieve the business aim.

However, even if this is the final decision, it is not the end of the relevant questioning process. What, it still needs to be asked, about the woman herself? She may be well aware of her ability to do the job and feel very aggrieved to be passed over. And what about the message this gives to other women (and men) in the business? Will they feel confident that they will be treated fairly? Unless there is another job available, of comparable responsibility and status, in which the woman could contribute as well or better to the business it is most unlikely that the decision to exclude her from consideration for the original position would be the right one. Justice being done and being seen to be done is a fundamental of ethical business practice. Fair dealing is the basis of ethical employee relations.

Even if the judgement is that the solidarity of the team should be preserved and the female employee moved elsewhere, the longer-term implications of this decision need to be faced. How does this small team's culture fit in with the values of the rest of the organisation? If they are perceived to be at odds with the public statements of management on equal opportunities, for example, is this not undermining of the business's position here? Will existing employees and potential recruits not rightly look askance at the protestations and the reality? And how does the business deal with the next vacancy in the group? What if the most suitable candidate this time is not a woman but a man who happens not to share the attitudes and sense of humour of the group? Without having thought through such questions, the business leaves itself open to charges of unethical conduct and of failure to achieve its own best interests in its human resource management.

TRAINING

The same basic principles already identified inform the decisions about training in the ethical organisation. The aim of training should be to give employees the skills and experience to do the job the business asks them to do. Businesses can and do improve the skills of employees into a significant competitive advantage. In any business where a commodity or service is offered, for example, often the most important point of differentiation between producers is the quality of their staff, which will depend heavily on the quality of their training. And the process is often self-reinforcing: a reputation for good training will attract good people who are in themselves a considerable business asset.

There are two issues commonly raised against this view of the place of training and its business advantages. The first is that training cannot simply be about economic performance; it is and ought to be also about personal development. The second is that training is a liability rather than a business asset. It costs businesses dearly and its returns are, at best, uncertain. The first point is clearly expressed in the following comment:

> Surely the point about training is much deeper than economic perform-ance ... Training, just like education, is concerned with the growth and development of the individual, the capacity of the individual to contribute more to society and to gain more in return through a fuller sense of contribution. Self-betterment, enhanced capacity to give and grow – *these* are what training is about.'[15]

The business aim, however, is not the 'self-betterment' of employees in the spiritual or existential sense. It is true that well-trained people will almost certainly have a better feeling about their capacity to do their job well and probably, therefore, a better feeling about themselves. But this is not the aim of training, which remains that of giving employees the skills and experience to do, as well as possible, the jobs the business asks them to do.

And the distinction is important. If the aim of training were simply to enhance personal well-being, the business could be well advised to look at replacing its quality management pro-gramme or its retail and marketing training with encounter group sessions or compulsory yoga two nights a week for all grades. And this is not to be glib or dismissive of the importance of group activity for some companies. Many highly successful Japanese businesses, for example, encourage company-wide participation in daily physical exercise as much for the 'bonding' among staff

---

[15] P. Ashby, A training revolution?, *St George's House Annual Review*, 1990, p. 21.

which such activity involves as for its presumed cardio-vascular advantages. They do not, however, suggest this as an alternative to training and nor should any business which looks to fulfil its aim.

The second question, whether training pays or not, is often raised by business people. The costs of training are obvious and identifiable; the advantages may be less clear and calculable. Training may sometimes appear to be a very expensive act of faith and it is quite understandable that smaller companies in particular are unsure of its value. 'I spend on training as little as I can get away with because I cannot afford to do more' is the typical comment of a small business manager, who goes on, 'The training must pay me as an employer and I must not squander the resources of my . . . organisation on it.'[16] Very true: but how can we show unequivocally that 'training pays'? It rather depends on what you mean by 'pays', on what the opportunity costs are and what your timescale is. If training has to show a clear and immediate contribution through to the bottom line, then it may be difficult to show that it 'pays'. On the other hand, many companies with excellent records in attaining their business targets time after time – Hewlett Packard, Marks and Spencer and Nissan are examples – are convinced that their business objectives are well served by good training. A recent report from Hay Management Consultants also suggests that being able to offer good training is one of the most effective ways of attracting and retaining good people.[17] And although the small business may say that big concerns can afford to invest here but they cannot, the real question may be whether they can afford not to. It is the larger companies, after all, which provide the exemplary culture, and set the standards and the expectations of the future. Successful international competition is often about creating and maintaining quality and this can only be done by training and maintaining a quality workforce.[18] And increasingly

[16] Hilary Steedman in Towards a quality workforce, *RSA Journal*, vol. 139, May 1991, p. 384.
[17] Quoted in S. Carmichael and J. Drummond, *Good Business*, Business Books, 1989, p. 39.
[18] Quality is becoming a crucial factor in international competitiveness. For the relationship between quality and training, see Where training has pride of place, *The Independent*, 7 May 1991, p. 21.

employees expect to be trained and will gravitate towards those businesses which take training seriously and will give them the tools to do a good job and therefore to take pride in it.

If remuneration (pay, bonuses and perks) is taken to be central to the incentive system of businesses, this must be on the assumption that people are motivated to some extent by money. One need not agree, however, that, as the saying goes, 'if a man says it's not the money but the principle of the thing – it's the money'. There is a fair amount of research to suggest that people are motivated by many other things than direct financial compensation.[19] Benefits, like cheap mortgages or a company car or subsidised canteen food, may be incentives. So may bonuses paid on the achievement of an Open University degree (Thomas Cook offer this) or share options at a price below the market rate (Cadbury Schweppes offer these).[20]

Even further away from financial returns, in money or in kind, is the offer of the fulfilment of a fantasy or dream – a week at a five-star hotel for the 'salesman of the year' or a chance to drive the boss's Rolls Royce for the manager and staff of the best-performing shop in the chain. This latter is one of the incentives offered by Richer Sounds, a small specialist hi-fi business. The owner, Julian Richer, believes that such incentives help explain why his staff turnover is minimal and his profits so healthy.[21]

Not all remuneration, then, need be financial. As the huge corpus of literature on organisational behaviour shows, people are motivated by a great many things but most fundamentally, perhaps, by the desire to be treated fairly. Feeling that they have been reasonably rewarded for their efforts is crucially important to people's self-esteem. To be fairly paid in relation to other people within the business and also to those doing similar work elsewhere is the basic requirement here. Consequently, people may feel as uncomfortable if they believe they

---

[19] See for example, D. McLaughlin in F. K. Foulkes, *Executive Compensation, A Strategic Guide for the 1990s*, Harvard Business School Press, 1991.
[20] Golden hello or gilt handcuffs, *The Times*, 30 October 1989, p. 13.
[21] Feeling Richer for being rewarded, *The Financial Times*, 5 February 1991, p. 13.

are being paid too much as if they think they are are paid too little.[22]

The basis of remuneration in the ethical organisation should be distributive justice. This requires that the system be based on the *recognition of value to the business*. Further, it is necessary that the criteria on which such judgements are made should be *clear and publicly available*, and that they are impersonally or *objectively applied*.

Fair remuneration demands, in other words, that people are paid according to their contribution to the business and not according to other criteria such as, for example, being a good and caring human being or the brother-in-law of the chairman or head of a one-parent family. (If the business needs to attract and/or retain staff in certain categories, of course, it may offer inducements like flexible working hours or retraining packages, but the criterion here is whether the business aim is served rather than the private qualities or interests of particular individuals.)

The criteria need to be clear and publicly available so that people can see what they are meant to be aiming for and focus their efforts on achieving it. The alternative, where aims are uncertain or constantly seem to be changing, is deeply counter-productive. During the 1980s restructuring of the universities in the UK, for example, there was a strong feeling among academics that the goalposts were constantly being changed and that what they were being asked to do was unclear and priorities indistinct. The publicly available criteria for promotion became, in this context, singularly unhelpful. (Should a young hopeful pursue academic excellence in research or get out into the marketplace as a consultant and sell his/her skills? Was teaching more important than publications – or was administrative ability more important than either?) The resultant confusion led to what looked like arbitrariness and unfairness which in turn contributed heavily to the general demoralisation of the profession.

The objective application of the criteria, once identified, is obviously crucial too. The decision as to whether A or B has contributed more to the business may be a matter of judgement but it can never, justly, be a matter of whim or personal self-interest.

There are two sets of judgements which need to be made in establishing a remuneration system which is seen as fair. The first

---

[22] See for example, E. Lawler, *Pay and Organisational Effectiveness*, McGraw Hill, 1971.

is between different jobs in the organisation – the chairman is generally paid more than the doorman. The second is how well a job at any particular level is done – the 'salesman of the year' is paid more than his colleagues. In the first case, although it can fairly be said that everyone in the business makes a contribution to it, it would probably be accepted by most people that some contributions are more fundamental to the business's success than others. The business might well survive more easily without the doorman than without the chairman and it could certainly replace the doorman with less difficulty than the chairman. Judged in terms of their value to the business, then, it would not seem unreasonable or unjust to pay the latter more than the former.

Making distinctions in such obvious and generalised terms is not too difficult. The real problems arise when contributions are recognised as disparate but seen as nearer in value for the business. Should the finance director be paid more than a salesman? Both are important to the business; both deserve to be rewarded. Again, however, the chances are that it will be easier for the business to find another salesman than another finance director. But if sales are central to what this business is about, the remuneration system should reflect this in the bonuses it pays, and the supersalesman may well earn more than the finance director in the end.

Bonuses and commissions are a way of recognising that some people work harder or are more talented and therefore produce more for the business than others. They allow the recognition and reward of achievement, whether of the individual or, more often these days, of the group. Bonuses, like pay, must relate to business performance, be measurable and objectively applied. They must, if they are to be ethical, be a reward for achieving identifiable business goals and never a way of, for example, compensating for a low basic salary.

The basis of all remuneration should be a commonly agreed standard of justice and fairness within the business and an appreciation by everyone that individual interests are, in the long run, normally best served by being seen in the context of achieving the business aim. Ray Stata, Chairman and CEO of Analog Devices, an American semi-conductor company, puts the notion elegantly:

A framework for compensation grows out of what the partners in a corporation believe to be its purpose. A corporation is a voluntary association of people ... who share a common long-term interest in the success of the firm ... When such partners are motivated by enlightened self-interest, they do not seek short-term gratification ... but look for an integrated plan for long-term success and happiness. The interests of the employee and the company coincide, since the individual's long-term career goals can be achieved best when the business is strong and healthy.[23]

REDUNDANCY – Surplus to requirements

No business can welcome having to make some of its employees redundant but, for a number of reasons, this may become necessary. The focus of a business may change, requiring different skills from the workforce; or recession may mean volumes are down and with them jobs; or the business may simply cease to be viable altogether because of changes in the macro-economic situation. The only permanancy in business is change and this will sometimes mean job losses.

Employees do, of course, have rights in law to a certain period of notice, to consultation through their unions, to redundancy payments and so on, as specified in, for example, the Employment Protection (Consolidation) Act 1978, the Employment Acts 1980 and 1982 and the Wages Act 1986.[24] However, as usual for the ethical organisation, the law is simply the basic minimum to which the business must conform in such situations. It says little or nothing about the attitudes which should inform the relations of the business with its employees in this situation.

Do businesses have an obligation to employees when their skills are no longer needed or when the company faces recession or shrinking demand? Charles Handy, for example, argues that managers, at least, are professionals who 'now believe in transferable skills and resent patronage and paternalism'.[25] And he goes on to say that earnings will 'increasingly be related to marketable skills, redundant skills will be cut from payrolls, organisations will feel less obligation towards their managers'. However, one need not be paternalistic to believe that the business has to ask itself some important questions about its attitude to people whom,

[23] *The Financial Times*, 27 February 1991, p. 15.
[24] For a useful simplified summary of employment legislation and employee rights, see the Department of Employment pamphlets (prepared by the Central Office of Information), PL707, PL712, PL756 and PL808, HMSO, various dates.
[25] C. Handy, *Understanding Organisations*, Penguin Books, 3rd edition, 1985, p. 382.

for whatever reason, it can no longer employ, even if these people are apparently tough and independent managers.

To begin at the beginning again is to remind ourselves of the business aim. The business is not in business to give people a job for life. That said, the possibility of increasing long-term shareholder value is greatly enhanced by a workforce which is treated and which is seen to be treated with decency and fairness. Once again then, these values will be the central ones to apply in the event of job losses.

In a situation which is obviously extremely stressful and difficult for most people, it is important that the business does not add to its problem by inept or insensitive handling of the process. Central to this is the clarity and truthfulness of information given to the workforce and therefore openness must be added to the values of decency and fairness identified above. The business aim is the creation of *long-term* owner value. It must be clear, then, if a decision is taken to make some of the workforce redundant, that an inappropriately short-term view has been avoided. Laying people off, it may even be thought temporarily, can seem an easy way of saving money. Costs are cut, budgets met and the business lives to fight another day. Like cutting training or R&D, it may seem like a good or even the only possible scheme at the time, but the costs may only become obvious at a later date. The loss of trained people is a permanent loss; the loyalty of remaining staff may be undermined as they wonder what is in store for them next; and the direct costs can be enormous as people claim the redundancy pay and time off to which they are entitled by law. Other ways of cutting costs, difficult or uncomfortable as they may be, should always be considered before redundancy.

In law, employers have a duty to consult with unions whenever they propose to make even a single person redundant. The employer has to give reasons for the proposals, the numbers and types of employees involved, how employees are to be selected for dismissal and within what timescale. It is then up to the unions to reply and to offer any objections or alternative suggestions, to which the employer must respond. If the suggested alternatives are rejected, reasons must be given.

Even if it is the initial judgement of the employer that redundancies must go ahead, it is important that the consultation should be a real one and not merely shadow play. Merely going through the motions will undermine trust in the good faith of the management, not only among those who are to lose their jobs and among remaining employees, but among other stakeholders who may be uncertain of the management's tactics. This is not to suggest that all redundancy decisions are wrong. The alternatives may have been exhaustively considered and the decision may still inevitably come back to job losses.

In which case, the question is how this can be done with as little damage as possible. Writing about Machiavelli, Sheldon Wolin commends the sixteenth-century master of intrigue not for his murderous self-interest but for his advocacy of the 'economy of violence'.[26] Once a decision was taken, said Machiavelli, the trick was to minimise the amount of blood on the walls. This was best for all concerned but it often took considerable skill to avoid excessive pain and waste.

To be ethical, it is not the case that a business may never fire people. Indeed, it may be absolutely necessary to get rid of some of the workforce to secure the future of the remainder. To take the decision not to fire would in that case be not ethical but cowardly. The decision having been taken, however, it should be put into practice as far as possible openly, decently and justly. Openness, in participation with, for example, unions, has already been mentioned. It also involves keeping staff as far as possible up to date on what decisions are being taken so that rumour and uncertainty are avoided. This is not in any sense the easy path for those remaining in the business. When Marks and Spencer decided, in the spring of 1991, to make several hundred people redundant, the company was praised for the generosity of its pay-offs. Yet, as Richard Greenbury, the chairman, points out, it was 'very painful. It is one thing to talk about these things but it is quite another to face someone you know and like across a desk and say you are no longer needed.'[27] The company also made it very clear to remaining employees that no more staff cuts were planned and that the company welfare programme would be protected into the future. The redundancy decision was

---

[26] S. Wolin, *Politics and Vision: Continuity and Innovation in Western Political Thought*, Allen & Unwin, 1960, p. 221.
[27] Quoted in *The Financial Times*, weekend 18/19 May 1991, p. 12.

clearly damaging to staff morale but it might have been more so if uncertainty and rumour had not been promptly dealt with.

Human decency may seem hard to define in such a context but it is easy to recognise. When it is upheld in the difficult circumstances of redundancy, it says much about the business to its stakeholders, including employees. British Coal is operating in an area, coal mining, which is still going through large-scale industrial restructuring with resultant job losses in parts of the country where other sources of employment are scarce. In 1984, it set up British Coal Enterprise with the object of creating 'new alternative job opportunities in the coal mining regions of Britain'.[28] An important part of the strategy is to place redundant workers from British Coal and elsewhere in new employment in the area, while employers locating or expanding locally can be helped to assemble their management team and workforce. The impact of such a scheme on employees, both past and present, is not hard to imagine in a business where there is more than usual uncertainty about the future. Thus the business gains in stability and loyalty by providing a service which recognises the human costs of redundancy and treats employees with decency.

Justice and fairness can be reflected in many ways in the course of a redundancy action. Everything from the size of redundancy payments to the order of lay-offs should reflect as far as possible the contributions of the individuals to the business (and indeed some such decisions are directed in this way by law). There is nothing inherently unjust about redundancy itself in a market economy. At least in theory, the human resource which is unemployable or inefficiently employed in one context will be efficiently employed in another. In practice, of course, the situation is often a good deal more complicated than this and the human and emotional toll of redundancy has to be recognised by any business which takes employee interests seriously – which means any long-term successful business. The justice with which the process is carried out and is seen to be carried out is critical in determining how well the business survives into the future.

MOTIVATION OR MANIPULATION?

In recruitment, remuneration and redundancy, a business will try to identify what motivates individuals and will attempt to

---

[28] Backing business, making jobs, *British Coal Enterprise Annual Review*, 1990–1, p. 1.

influence them accordingly. Is this, as Charles Handy asks, manipulation – or management?[29] To pose the question thus is perhaps confusing since it suggests that management is nothing but manipulation by another name. Yet the point is well made that many people do mistrust the impulse to motivate people at work as manipulative and therefore unethical.

At one level, this is a variant of the confusion we pointed to in chapter 3 where the concern was whether if something was good for the business, it could be ethical. If good employee relations are good for the business, can *they* be ethical? This is again to assimilate moral good entirely to good intentions and to give no significance to good outcomes.

However, the attempt to understand the springs of satisfaction at work is, it can surely be argued, a necessary prerequisite of taking better, more informed business decisions, with all the implications that has for employees as for others associated with the business. This is not manipulation but merely good practice. If people see themselves as manipulated, if they know they are being used, this will be severely counter-productive. Justice and common decency are the values to which most people respond, not because they are manipulated by them but because they resonate to the attempt by others to be just and decent. As Tom Peters endlessly points out, there are some things you can't fake and integrity is one of them.[30] Or as Aristotle would have it, how do you have integrity? By consistently acting with integrity. There is no trick and if there were, employees would spot it instantly.

---

[29] Handy, *Understanding Organisations*, p. 26.
[30] T. Peters and N. Austin, A Passion for Excellence, Random House, 1985, p. 261.

5

Finance

... the poor stockholder is the one whose interest is being ignored in favour of the egos of directors and executives. And who the hell is running the show ... while all of this is going on?

(Bendix director during the Bendix/Martin Marietta takeover battle)

The vulture has a place in nature.

(plc board member, talking about corporate raiders)

The old-fashioned idea that decent banks only deal with decent customers serves both sides in the relationship.

(Hamish McRae, City Editor, *The Independent*)

Money makes the business world go round, of that there is no doubt. Without finance, there is no business, or at least there is no possibility of acquisition of tangible assets such as plant and machinery, no development of technological innovation, no training of employees and increase in the knowledge base, no growing of the market. Money is, as has often been said, itself neither good nor bad. Its mere existence is not an ethical issue. In business, similarly, the existence of capital markets is not an ethical issue, even if these are sometimes presented as a cross between a casino and a thieves' den. The ethical issues involved in finance are not, therefore, about the morality of the market, although one could be forgiven for thinking they were when one hears some commentators' views. Listen to Robert Kuttner, for example, writing in The *New Republic*: '[T. Boone] Pickens and (Irwin) Jacobs make their livings borrowing money and attempting to seize control of corporations, or cashing in their shares for a fast profit once they have set off a bidding war.'[1]

---

[1] R. Kuttner, The truth about corporate raiders, *The New Republic*, 20 January 1986, quoted in M. Hoffman and J. Moore, *Business Ethics*, McGraw-Hill, p. 240.

The implication here is that debt is suspect, taking control of businesses is only for the power-crazed, and profits, particularly if you don't have to wait for them, are ethically uncertain. Yet there is nothing inherently unethical about borrowing money; without it, most business ventures would simply not be possible. Again, taking control of a business which has been poorly managed may simply be a way of releasing assets which have been underutilised and giving a better return to the owners: there is nothing unethical about that. And profits, even short-term profits, are the required rewards of business enterprise, without which there would be no business. Again, there is no immorality attached to profits unless business itself is to be categorised as unethical.

The ethical issues associated with finance are not, therefore, centrally concerned with the morality of making money but much more with *why* and *how* money is made. The criterion for all financial decision-making must, as ever, be the securing of long-term owner value, not the desire for personal power or saving the jobs of the board or the fashion for acquisition or short-term gain. If the aim of the business is borne in mind all the time, many issues which seem, on the face of it, to involve intractable ethical dilemmas may turn out to be largely the result of confusions about that aim.

THE ETHICAL QUESTIONS

But it might still be thought that the fundamental ethical questions here involve the morality of the financial market itself, its mechanisms, assumptions and expectations. And the way in which questions about the market are sometimes phrased may increase this impression. For example, is making a profit or charging interest morally acceptable? But although these may be questions for moral philosophy, they cannot be the main preoccupation of business ethics. Just as business ethics assumes the existence of business and does not try to justify it or condemn it as an activity, so it assumes the existence of the various activities which make up business. Making a profit is not illegal or against regulation and it is integral to doing business. Business ethics is concerned not with the justification or otherwise of the activity as such, but with how and why it is done – with regard to justice and common decency or not, and to achieve the business aim rather than to fulfil some personal whim or ambition.

Sometimes, too, issues are raised in such general terms as to be virtually meaningless. 'Are hostile takeovers a good thing?' is, as it stands, a contextless abstraction. The ethical implications, the rights and wrongs of takeovers, can only be sensibly explored when the question has been unpacked and possible backgrounds to the activity sketched in.

As in other areas, compliance with the law is not the same as ethical action. For example, directors have a fiduciary duty to care for the assets of the business on behalf of the owners of the business. Such legal requirements will generally be met by the ethical organisation but their fulfilment is not necessarily the end of its ethical obligation. It is the case too that, although fraud is indeed unethical (normally involving lying, cheating and stealing), it is also illegal and will be dealt with more often by preferring charges than by invoking codes of ethics.

The fundamental ethical questions in relation to finance, then, are to do with conflicts of interests and perceptions of responsibility. All sorts of conflicts of interest may emerge in the course of making financial arrangements but the most common is possibly that of management versus owners, where the existence of the management is threatened by a change which the owners think will be to their advantage. Is there loyalty owed here? If so, by whom to whom? By both to each other? If there is a conflict of interest, whose interest should be paramount? We will try to look at these questions in relation especially to takeovers and management buy-outs.

How far and for what different groups take responsibility is another important issue raised in relation to finance. The responsibilities of boards is dealt with in greater detail in the chapter on corporate governance but will be touched on here in looking at the board's role in mergers and acquisitions, investment decisions, accounting and auditing practices, etc. The responsibilities of lenders will be explored in looking at the position of the banks. Should they owe a duty of care to borrowers or does the principle of *caveat emptor* apply as much to buying money as to other goods and services? The responsibilities of professionals too, of accountants and auditors, is a topical and thorny question. They may face conflicts of interest in their

it is the buyers responsibility to satisfy himself about the quality of the goods he receives relations with the shareholders whom they serve and the boards who employ them. Again, there are clear overlaps here with corporate governance but in this chapter we will try to deal with the principles more than the structures conducive to ethical action.

SHORT TERM *v* LONG TERM: CONFLICT OF INTEREST?

The notion of 'short-termism' covers a multitude of sins. It is always used in a pejorative sense, implying a lack of judgement, an unwillingness or inability to take the longer view and an unacceptable desire to make a fast buck. It is used to castigate anyone who is looking for a quicker payback on their investment than those who criticise them: by industry of the City, who, they say, will not give them the time they need for important projects to succeed; by managements who say that shareholders, analysts and fund managers are always breathing down their necks for quick returns; or by boards who feel held to ransom by shareholders who will otherwise succumb to the advances of any paying-out predator.[2] Specifically, businesses often believe that capital markets misprice shares, largely because of their emphasis on current earnings, without any longer term view. This leads to price/earnings ratios being applied to figures which are initially too low because they don't take account of the long-term earning potential of capital investment or R&D. Also, it is frequently pointed out, fund managers, who represent the big institutional shareholders, are evaluated on their quarterly performance and may well, therefore, have horizons limited to the next three months.

The debate becomes wider, too, when the City's response to business's accusations is to characterise business itself as short-termist. It is not the case that shares are mispriced or that price/earnings ratios fail to reflect longer term prospects – indeed, they say, share prices often increase following the announcement of (long-term) research and development programmes or large investments in capital spending. It is not the capital markets but

---

[2] On the debate on short-termism, see for example, Short-termism: myth or reality?, *Financial Times*, 11 February 1991, p. 9. Also, Why perception and reality do not tally, *Financial Times*, 22 July 1991, p. 9.

businesses which react to pressures to increase dividends rather than make capital or research investments; it is business which takes the short-term view and the only remedy for this is for management to raise their sights and 'manage as if tomorrow mattered'.[3]

Whatever the truth of the situation, and it is clearly complex and many-faceted, capital markets have obviously moved on from the simple role of providing capital for business; they are predominantly concerned now with the trading of stocks for capital gain. And those who trade in the market are less concerned with their role as 'owners' of shares in a business enterprise than in the diversification of their 'risk' and the performance of their overall portfolios against an index.

In such a context, it is all too easy for businesses to lose sight of their aim and to respond merely to the short-term volatility of the market. But the business aim is the production of long-term owner value which means that management must manage 'as if tomorrow mattered', precisely because it does. If business is without this clear view of its own direction, it will be likely to drift with City priorities. Quick paybacks are no more an acceptable criterion for business decision-taking than is the desire of the board for greater personal power or prestige.

TAKEOVERS — FRIENDLY AND HOSTILE, INTERNAL AND EXTERNAL

If management and boards were genuinely accountable to owners who, in turn, were clear about their own interests and willing to assert them, takeovers would be less common and less necessary. That, at any rate, is the theory. A change of ownership would not be the best way to deal with bad management or to release underused assets in a business. But, at the moment, so the argument goes, lack of direct management accountability means that a merger or acquisition, achieved either in a friendly way or by force, by management themselves or by an outside raider, is the only way in which the market can assert itself and the interests of shareholders be protected.

What is the *ethical* problem at the heart of the takeover debate?

[3] *Financial Times*, 22 July 1991, p. 9.

It is to do with the reasons behind takeover decisions. Takeovers have got a bad name for many reasons but the most compelling ethical criticism is that they have not been undertaken in further-ance of the business aim. Where mergers and acquisitions (M& A) become a way of life, for example, an unthinking reflex action which replaces strategic direction in a business, the outcomes are likely to be unsatisfactory in the longer term. Morgan Gren-fell, the merchant bank, went with the M&A trend of the 1980s to the extent that its business in that area rose from £1 billion per annum to over £15 billion, by which time M&A's revenue contribution was 32 per cent of that of the business as a whole.[4] The outcome of following fashion here, rather than taking decisions which protected or ensured the longer term interests of the business, was involvement, in 1986, in the disastrous Guinness takeover of Distillers. Although the company was not directly prosecuted, heads rolled in the corporate finance depart-ment and Morgan Grenfell ceased trading on the securities market in 1988, costing the jobs of some 400 employees. The errors here were not just errors of judgement about which merger to back and how much to lend; they were, in the end, errors of principle. The strategic direction of the business had been lost; decisions were not taken in the long-term interests of the owners of the business. Fashion prevailed and the business was the loser.

'When you buy another company, you are making an invest-ment and the basic principles of capital investment decisions apply. You should go ahead with the purchase if it makes a net contribution to shareholders' wealth.'[5] Thus goes the textbook account of the rationale behind acquisition. To act in such a way is to act as a business. This means, of course, that many factors other than simply the direct financial costs and benefits of the transaction will have to be considered. Long-term value is dependent on employee morale, on supplier relations, on customer perceptions; it is dependent too on the limitation of personal greed and egoism by those making investment decisions. Just as fashion is no grounds for takeover, neither is boredom or the desire for self-publicity of those at the helm, or the need for huge

---

[4] D. Hobson, *The Pride of Lucifer: The Unauthorised Biography of a Merchant Bank*, Hamish Hamilton, 1989.
[5] R. Brealey and S. Myers, *Principles of Corporate Finance*, McGraw-Hill, 1988, p. 793.

fees for their legal and financial advisors. The biggest takeover
in American business history was that of RJR Nabisco, the US
food and tobacco group, by Kohlberg Kravis Roberts for $25
billion. The saga began with the attempted purchase of RJR,
apparently a fairly healthy company, if run more for the benefit
of the management than the owners, by its own chief executive.
The story goes that he bid for it, hoping to take it over on the
cheap, so setting off a series of counter-bids in a scramble for
control of the company. The company was left with new owners
but little in the way of changed shareholder value, except perhaps
the debt, running into billions, which was raised to fund the
takeover in the first place.[6]

The RJR Nabisco case is a good example of the conflicts of
interests involved in many takeovers. The RJR board was mainly
concerned to protect itself and maintain control. This it tried to
do by leverage, so that it acquired a huge burden of debt. This
meant, in turn, that, since these moves were seen by the financial
markets much more as banking transactions than as longer-term
equity investments, their concerns were with whether the company's short-term cash flows were sufficient to service the debt,
rather than with the longer term prospects of the cigarette and
food businesses. Again, there may seem to be a conflict between
the banker as professional, working for the good of his own
business, and the banker as *owner* of shares in a business and
not simply *trader* of shares. But the two can and must come
together; for the long-term interest of the lending business must
depend on the long-term health of the businesses in which it has
invested. The excesses of the RJR takeover can only be avoided
if the criterion of projects is clearly the achievement of the
aim of long-term owner value and the mechanisms for making
companies accountable to their shareholders are firmly in place.

Takeover bids instigated for reasons of fashion or self-
aggrandisement are perhaps all too obviously unethical. What
about situations where a business is the target of a bid which
the board believe to be unjustified in the sense that the bidder
has nothing to offer to the business, that experience is all with
the existing management and the shareholder is well served by

---

[6] B. Burrough and J. Hellyar, *Barbarians at the Gate: The Fall of RJR Nabisco*, Harper
and Row, 1989.

the present arrangements? On the face of it, if all these conditions were fulfilled, there would seem to be no further value to be squeezed out of the business simply by a change of ownership. But if the predator were contemplating a merger where there was synergy with their existing business, the takeover might make two plus two equal five – because of, for example, gains from economies of scale, the exploitation of tax advantages or the advantages of vertical integration. In such a case, what is the duty of the board of the target company?

In many cases, since the takeover rush began in the 1980s, boards don't wait for bids to be made before taking defensive action. They try to preempt the possibility of having to repel invaders by using various defences which make the business less attractive. They may, for example, give 'poison pill' rights to shareholders to buy bonds which, in the event of a merger, have to be repurchased by the acquiring firm. Or they may have two classes of shares, one with superior voting rights which, if distributed to management, allow them the greatest say (regardless of who owns the majority of the shares) as to the outcome of the bid. Or they may go for a 'supermajority', where a very high percentage – say, 80–90 per cent – of voting stock is needed to approve a takeover.

After a bid has been made, other defences can be offered by the target business. Litigation at this stage is not uncommon. In the USA, this will normally try and show that anti-trust regulations are being violated. In the UK, injunctions may be sought and the Monopolies and Mergers Commission (MMC) invoked. Again, the so-called 'Pacman' defence may be used by making a bid for the stock of the bidder, or assets of particular value to the bidder may be sold off to make the target less attractive (often referred to as 'selling the crown jewels'). Sometimes, too, boards will be 'greenmailed' into buying up the shares which the hostile bidder has acquired in the company for a premium, so that the bidder is satisfied and goes away.

The important question to ask in deciding on the acceptability of such tactics is why managers are contesting bids to take over their companies. It may be that they believe that the interests of their shareholders will genuinely be served if they, rather than the bidder, run the company; that they have the skills, experience and long-term strategy to add greater value for owners than any opposing management. They may also, of course, simply believe that their jobs will be at risk in the new company. Or again, they may believe that the takeover is ultimately a good thing for the owners but think that they can get a better price for the shares (there is evidence that contested takeovers produce a higher price for shares in the acquired company).

If the board is simply protecting itself, there is no ethical justification for its attempt to stop the merger. Some companies have tried to reduce the conflicting interests of management and shareholder here by offering 'golden parachutes' to their directors which guarantee them large pay-offs if they lose their jobs in the event of a takeover. This, of course, hardly deals at all with the ethical question, for individuals who are prepared to put their own interests before that of their shareholders in hanging onto their jobs are hardly likely to be any more reliably committed to them when it comes to losing their jobs for large cash incentives. The only way of ensuring that the right; thing is done, whether that means selling or hanging on, is to judge projects always by the criterion of the business aim. If the deal is productive of long-term value for owners it is right; if not, it is not. What about ethical principles here? As we have argued elsewhere, the basis of ethical action in business is being true to the business aim. It is on this basis that businesses employ people, take money from shareholders, set up relations with suppliers etc. What is fundamentally *unethical* is to operate under false pretences, to change your avowed aim (of being a business and not a society for the protection of the interests of the board or whatever) after people have committed themselves to you on that basis. The ethical principles of justice and decency follow on from this. Distributive justice is a necessary requirement for the achievement of the business aim and decency in the treatment of *all* stakeholders ensures that people are prepared to go on committing themselves to that aim.

The assertion of the business aim of achieving long-term owner value is not the same, of course, as identifying exactly what that aim involves in a particular situation. It is not always clear whether a proposed merger will contribute to long-term owner value and it will always be a matter for management judgement. The huge academic literature on mergers is somewhat ambivalent on the question of whether they generate net benefits. There seems to be general agreement that selling businesses gain from acquisition; it is uncertain whether the acquirer gains at all but it seems clear that any gain is less than for the seller.[7] From the point of view of business ethics, however, the establishment of the correct principles of action is what is important. The questions of the numbers must be left to the economists.

MANAGEMENT BUY-OUTS (MBOs)

From time to time, a company's management may band together to buy all or a part of a business to run it as a private company. Sometimes this is a way of revitalising an enterprise which has lost its strategic vision; sometimes it suits boards of large corporations to sell off a non-core business as a way of restructuring and many boards will now look favourably at the possibility of an MBO as an alternative to finding a corporate buyer. MBO activity has increased dramatically over the past decade and, according to Nottingham University's Centre for Management Buy-out Research, this has resulted, between 1982 and 1992, in deals worth some £26 billion. A very large chunk of UK venture capital – 55 per cent in 1991 – went on buy-out transactions and the overall European figure for the same period was 35 per cent.[8]

Supporters of MBOs claim that they release entrepreneurial spirit and give managers the incentive to cut costs and increase margins once they are working for themselves. It is suggested too that because so many MBOs are also leveraged buy-outs (LBOs), that is, they are financed less on equity capital than on heavy bank borrowing, this inclines the new owner-managers to put every effort into the business in order to service the debt.

That MBOs can be very successful, particularly in their first few years, seems to be confirmed by the results of research done by Warwick Business School which found that their sample of 58 MBOs performed better than the average of their industry.[9]

There are those, however, who are more sceptical about the

[7] Brealey and Myers, *Principles*, p. 817.
[8] *Financial Times* Survey, *Management buy outs*, 3 December 1992, p. 1.
[9] Quoted in the *Financial Times*, 31 January 1990.

value of MBOs, suggesting that they are simply a device for allowing a few executives to make a great deal of quick money. Those who take this line point to the large number of MBOs which, within a very few years, sell themselves off to another company, often for extremely high returns to the original managers. Premier Brands, for example, was bought by its management from its parent company Cadbury-Schweppes in 1986. The company was sold on to Hillsdown Holdings in 1989, as a result of which its nine directors shared some £150 million. Istel, the computer services company, took even less time to be sold on. The Rover car group accepted the Istel management offer of £35 million in 1987 and by 1989 the new company had been sold to AT&T for £180 million. These high returns reflect the structure of MBOs where, typically, managers provide some capital, on the basis of which they get a disproportionate share of the equity. Most of the capital, however, is raised in bank loans, and when the managers sell on, their returns are often much greater than any increase in the value of the business.

What are the ethical issues involved here? Not making money *per se* which, as Dr Johnson said, is a fairly harmless way of passing the time. Profit, as we have said before, is neither illegal nor unethical and he who bears the risk quite reasonably expects to make the return. And there can be great risk as the case of Response, the textile group, showed when they were unable to keep up payments on the loans they had taken on, only eighteen months before, to finance their buy-out from Coloroll. They went into receivership and their managers lost their stakes. Yet, there is certainly an ethical problem if the returns are somehow much greater than the risks borne. Justice demands that people are rewarded according to their contribution to the business aim. If managers, in taking a company private, increase the owner value long term, they deserve their reward. If the increases are very high, returns of millions may well not be out of place. But if the business aim is undercut by short-term policies which merely milk the company and undermine its future value, this is altogether different and ethically unacceptable.

It may also reasonably be asked why managers are taking the company private in the first instance. If they think they can increase margins and cut costs after an MBO, why aren't they doing it now? Do they not owe the company for which they work their loyalty and their best efforts to advance the business aim? Of course, in some cases, the business as currently structured may be impossible to run efficiently and the present owners may be unable or unwilling to do anything about it. Much-needed capital may only be forthcoming via the buy-out route. But it is worth asking why managers believe that, in this case, a change of ownership is the only way to release assets and make an ailing business profitable.

LEVERAGE AND JUNK BONDS

Many buy-outs are financed largely by debt, so that the gearing of the new company, that is its debt/equity ratio, is very high. When Isosceles bought Gateway, the UK food retailer, for example, it did so with £200 million of equity and £2.2 billion of debt – debt of nearly ten times its equity.[10] In the USA, the risk on a business's assets is sometimes so high that the debt security is not investment grade, that is, it does not qualify for one of the top four ratings from Moody's or Standard and Poor's rating service. Below investment grade, bonds are traded in the so-called *junk bond market*. From the late 1970s, the junk bond market expanded with a pool of investors willing to accept extremely high default risk in return for very high promised returns. Are junk bonds ethically acceptable? Put in this form, in the abstract, the question is almost impossible to answer. It will depend on the interpretation of the question: whether it is seen from the point of view of public policy, economics, politics, business or any number of other perspectives.

What might unacceptability mean here? That they are bonds with a below investment-grade rating? That people can make a lot of money from trading in them, provided they take the risk? If this is what is meant, the answer seems to be don't move into the junk market unless you can carry that risk. Are junk bonds of value financially? Again the question is ambiguous – of value to whom? To hostile bidders or management buyers or bankers or investors or market-makers? And of value for what? To revitalise ailing companies or perk up the economy as a whole?

In the end, such questions are only sensible in a context – in

[10] Catching colds, *The Economist*, 27 January 1990, p. 90.

the context of this business and this project at this time. If
investment in junk bonds is being considered, it is surely essential
to look at the balance of the portfolio. High returns involve high
risk: the question may be less about ethics than about professional
caution. Again, if one is looking at junk bonds as a method of
financing a project, the relevant question may be not whether
such financial instruments are ethically acceptable but whether
they are the best (or only?) means of financing the project.

The genuinely ethical questions associated with junk bonds
are to do with the risk to the business and the effects of possible
failure to repay very high levels of debt on the business and its
stakeholders – its employees, suppliers, shareholders, etc. The
risk of failure means the risk of lost jobs, unpaid bills, failed
capital. Yet if taking this risk is the only way the project can
be financed and people associated with the business know this
and are prepared to go forward on this basis, there is nothing
inherently unethical about proceeding. If the risk were transferred
to employees or banks or suppliers, however, while owners continued to take the returns, this would be unethical.

INSIDER DEALING

If junk bonds provoke much high-minded but confused ponti-
ficating about the ethics or otherwise of debt, insider dealing
often sparks off equal confusion about access to information.
Insider dealing involves using price-sensitive information, which
one acquires because of one's professional or other position, for
personal gain, or to pass on to another for personal gain. It is
not only unethical but it is also illegal. It is, however, difficult
to define and to prosecute (between 1980, when it was first
declared illegal, and 1990 only twelve successful prosecutions
were brought in the UK). The definition, in law, of insider
dealing is clear, demanding that a jury be satisfied that the
information received was price-sensitive; that the information was
actually passed to the defendant; that the defendant knew that
the information was confidential and price-sensitive; that the
defendant knew that the information was unpublished; and that
the defendant used the information to profit or to avoid loss.
The apparent clarity and specificity of this legal position, however, may make it difficult to prosecute, never mind to secure a

conviction. In US law, by comparison, there is no definition of insider dealing and convictions have been achieved on the basis of case law, which may give courts greater discretion.[11]

The problem of legal enforcement is compounded by the fact that it is not always easy to make the distinction between an acceptable and unacceptable 'insider'. Whatever the theory that there is open information in the markets, the reality must be that some people will know more than others. Professionals simply do know more than the man in the street about what is going on: this is, after all, their job and is largely what they are paid for. If everybody had exactly the same information at any one time, there would be no point in taking investment advice.

Just because so many people often do have access to price-sensitive information, if it does become clear that word has got around in advance of a public announcement, it can be difficult to identify the source. For example, when Kingfisher, the British retail conglomerate, launched a bid for Dixons, the electrical business, in late 1989, some four hundred merchant bankers, accountants, lawyers and other professional advisors knew about the move at least forty-eight hours before it took place.[12] Dixon's shares jumped on the rumour of the bid and Kingfisher was forced to go public early on its bid intentions.

Such 'slippage' of confidential information may not be intentional, far less criminal. It may be a matter of indiscretion, of one person or several people saying individually innocent things which, when put together, make an interesting story for the already well-informed.

But there are also individuals who know exactly what they are doing in using information which comes their way in the course of their jobs. Loyalty is part of common decency within corporate ethics and preserving confidentiality is an important part of corporate loyalty. The individual who is determined to use confidential information for gain, however, will do so regardless of codes of conduct. As Michael Feltham, who was head of the Stock Exchange's insider-dealing investigation group, says, 'The simple fact is that there is a percentage of people who will misuse

[11] This has mainly been by successive interpretations of the phrase 'fraudulent means' as used in the 1933 Securities Act.
[12] How insiders slip the net, *Sunday Times*, 14 January 1990, p. E3.

information if they are given the opportunity.'[13] The danger of
such activity to the business community as a whole is in the
undermining of confidence and, in the City in particular, to the
undermining of assumptions of confidentiality and professionalism. The business aim itself is impossible to achieve without the
upholding of such confidence and confidentiality. At the end of
the biggest insider-dealing trial in Britain, in the summer of
1992, the judge spoke of the damage done not only to other
investors or potential investors in the City but to the financial
community and to the public as a whole.[14] Insider dealing is
illegal as well as unethical and it is therefore tempting to say
that this is not a concern primarily of business ethics. But
although ethics is not *the same as* the law, there is not a total
disjunction between the two. Business ethics, in analysing the
activity and its context, can show why insider dealing is both
counter-productive to business as a whole and *wrong* in ethical terms.
If clearly articulated value statements here cannot eliminate cor-
ruption, they can at the very least set the tone within which
business is done. Employees are not simply thrown back on their
own resources as to what are acceptable and unacceptable modes
of operation. 'Just do it – and we don't care how', even if only
the implicit message, is a dangerous background for any firm
operating in the market. But the ethical organisation cannot
simply reject such a *laissez-faire* approach; it must positively
identify its own standards and values and emphasise that it is
not just getting the contract but getting the contract without
ignoring the justice and decency that matters to the business in
the longer term.

BANKING

Banks are businesses too. They lend money which finances other
businesses in order to make a return for their shareholders and
protect the funds of their depositors. For a long time, banks were
seen as the very acme of probity and ethical acceptability; their
business was socially necessary, well based and safe – as safe as
the Bank of England. Over the past few years, however, this

[13] Insiders, *Sunday Times*.
[14] *Financial Times*, 10 June 1992, p. 20.

view has been eroded and the reputation and standing of the banks has been put in question. The charges laid against the banks are of unjust and indeed exploitative treatment of their customers, irresponsibility in their underwriting of debt and failure to blow the whistle on financially suspect or even corrupt individuals or organisations.

Particularly in the case of small businesses, the first claim is that very high interest rates, bank charges and the demand for collateral are all significant constraints on development. But just what is a bank's duty here? It is not in the business of government, of implementing a public policy of industrial expansion, say, by underwriting the risks on business development regardless of the exposure of the bank itself. On the other hand, it is in the business of lending money for a return and to be entirely risk-averse in such a business is to be unable to deliver the business aim of sustaining longer term owner value. Bank interest rates and charges should be a fair reflection of the risk of the loan.

Banks, it is sometimes suggested, are not only risk-averse; they are also monopolistic. They set rates in common, if not in concert, which means that there is no real market here and no point in shopping around. The customer takes what is offered, in both rates and service.

If this were the case, it would be illegal as well as unethical. A recent study carried out by a team from Nottingham University, however, found that it was not the case that banks did not pass on base rate cuts to their customers.[15] They also noted considerable differences in the quality of services provided by different banks to small businesses – the Scottish banks being more highly rated here than their English counterparts and Barclays and the National Westminster coming well ahead of Lloyds and the Midland. There is not, it would seem, necessarily a cartel in service provision. In spite of these findings, it was still the view of small businesses that the banks' quality of service had declined between 1990 and 1993.[16]

The answer to these concerns is to be found not in the uncritical

---

[15] The Forum of Private Business, Small Businesses and their Banks, reported in *Financial Times*, 19 January 1993, p. 11.
[16] ibid.

provision of financing to any who ask for it; that would be unbusinesslike and, in the end, unethical; but in the careful consideration of individual business projects rather than blanket high interest rates and a policy of swift foreclosures.

If the banks are sometimes represented as being too close-fisted, they are equally often accused of irresponsibility in their lending. Do banks have responsibilities to borrowers? Should people be able to take on as much credit as they can raise without the lending institutions being prepared to suggest any limits to what borrowers can afford? The business answer is relatively straight-forward, at least in theory. Banks are in the lending business; they are not debt counselling agencies. But they are, as businesses, committed to protecting their assets and there is no return for them, for example, in lending more to an organisation which is already putting all its cash flow into servicing existing debt. It is not that banks should second-guess customers' ability to take on another mortgage or repay that rate of interest, but they should and must make professional judgements about the security of their loan. The banks do not have a responsibility to remove the customer's responsibility; they do, however, have a responsibility to give the appropriate professional advice in the circumstances.

Investors and depositors in banks also have responsibilities which cannot and should not be entirely underwritten. When the American Bank of New England collapsed in 1991, its depositors with balances above the $100,000 legal limit were paid off by the federal authorities. This was done largely because the US banking system was, at the time, in a fragile condition where any collapse was thought likely to cause wider damage. But the danger of this kind of action is that it removes the incentive for depositors to be responsible and, indeed, for bank management to be tight and professional. Instead of looking for creditworthiness, depositors can simply look for the highest returns, in the knowledge that, if the bank goes under, their money will still be returned in full. This incentive for irresponsible behaviour created by insurance has been dubbed 'moral hazard'.[17]

Both borrowers and lenders need to subscribe to an ethical code which encourages discipline and responsibility rather than

[17] Moral hazard in New England, *Financial Times*, 8 January 1991.

taking it away. Being aware of greater risk encourages responsibility and depositors, therefore, should only be offered insurance to a certain level. A bank's record, too, should perhaps inform more directly its insurance premiums, thus keeping management's eyes more firmly fixed on its business performance.

Once again, the espousal of ethical standards of justice, decency and responsibility will not stop illegality. Criminals are unlikely to be deterred by value statements. Yet clear ethical standards allow criminals to be seen for what they are. Talking about Maxwell's legacy, Hamish McRae writes: 'It is a salutary lesson: dealing with rotters gets you into trouble. The . . . idea that decent banks only deal with decent customers serves both sides in the relationship.'[18]

REGULATION AND SELF-REGULATION

The financial scandals of the last few years have led some people to question the tradition of self-regulation as practised in the City. In spite of the 1986 Financial Services Act and the establishment of the Securities and Investments Board (SIB), the City is still largely regulated by practitioners for practitioners. However, Andrew Large, the SIB's chairman, is on record as favouring more of 'an enforcement culture' within the system.[19] He may even be in favour of using the civil law against wrongdoers, rather as the American Securities and Exchange Commission (SEC) does to some effect.

Again, the issues raised here go somewhat beyond those of ethics itself. When laws or regulations, whose purpose is to facilitate good practice in financial dealings, are broken, in spirit or in letter, the outcomes are likely to be unethical as well as illegal. But such practices cannot be banned by ethical injunction alone; rather, if society believes that certain actions are unethical and ultimately uncontrollable without the force of law, it must surely legislate accordingly. If self-regulation with its sanctions of peer group pressure and threat of ostracism from the financial community are not strong enough to control behaviour here,

[18] H. McRae, To be stupid is one thing, to be immoral is worse, *The Independent*, 17 June 1992.
[19] *Financial Times*, 3 November 1992, p. 15.

then tougher and more direct penalties must be put in place. Mr Large is concerned that 'the [existing] enforcement procedures are too complex and that punishments have not been enough'.[20] The minister with (as of 1994) responsibility for financial regulation, Anthony Nelson, apparently holds to much the same view when he says, 'I'm a believer in the power of fear . . . I want to be more intrusive, incisive, where necessary more penal.'[21]

Whatever happens, and Mr Large's report suggesting changes in City operations has not yet been presented to the government, it is likely that both regulatory frameworks and enforcement procedures will be much tightened. There is certainly a strong case for dealing with insider trading or other unfair and illegal ways of profiting from share price movements by methods other than the existing framework of the criminal law, if only because the level of proof required under the existing law on theft and fraud have proved to be unsuitable in such financial cases. In the last of the Guinness trials, for example, the long and costly proceedings led only (and no doubt correctly within the existing law) to acquittal.[22] If such cases were dealt with, as in America, through the civil courts (with their lower requirements on burden of proof) by the bodies set up to create the rules and monitor their observance, they might have much greater chances of successful prosecution and, importantly, recovery of assets. This would have the substantive effect of discouraging crooks by the reality of heavy fines and exclusion from further business dealings and would symbolically proclaim the City's commitment to its professional ethics. Some such clear commitment to underwriting ethical standards is essential if the financial markets are to continue to achieve their own business aim in maintaining the confidence of the whole business community.

[20] City self-regulation may erode, *Financial Times*, 2 November 1992, p. 18.
[21] Report in *Financial Times*, 4 December 1992.
[22] *The Times Law Report*, 16 February 1993.

6

Advertising and marketing

Humankind cannot bear very much reality.   (T. S. Eliot)

One cannot defend production as satisfying wants if that production creates the wants.   (J. K. Galbraith)

Life is not a spectacle but a predicament.   (St Augustine)

High-powered, hard-sell, glossy advertising is one of the most characteristic products of the late twentieth century. It seems, by the influence we ascribe to it and the seriousness with which we often judge it, almost a modern art form. From jingles to grand opera, from poster campaigns to television mini-sagas, anything may be pressed into service to sell everything from frozen peas to Prime Ministers. Advertising can be witty, intelligent, crude, offensive; it can make us laugh or even cry but it is aimed always at winning our support for the products it presents. Advertising may amuse us and brighten our lives but this is not its primary purpose, which is to sell. Vast sums of money are spent by businesses which believe that their success is largely dependent on their marketing and advertising, without which they think they would lose their competitive edge. Business uses advertising to convey information to consumers about its products. There would be no point in producing goods if nobody knew about them. Thus described, there hardly seems to be an ethical problem here: advertising is simply another way of securing long-term owner value.

WHAT IS THE QUESTION?

Yet there is often a general, if vague, unease with the whole area of marketing and advertising. This is frequently not very focused but is an amalgam of fears and uncertainties of different strengths and kinds and at various levels of philosophical abstraction, all characterised by the question 'Is advertising unethical?' But, just as we have suggested in earlier chapters, it may be worth asking whether this is, as it stands, a sensible question. What does it mean? Is advertising unduly materialistic? Does it encourage people to be greedy? Does it encourage thoughtless consumption and environmental depletion? Is it dishonest? Is it manipulative? Is it intrusive? Is it discriminatory? Is it distasteful? Is it unacceptable in terms of the individual or of society as a whole? Does it limit customer choice? Does it target the weak? These are just some of the questions which might lie behind the query about the morality of marketing in general and advertising in particular. It is worth beginning, then, by deciding what are the *ethical* issues at stake here, as opposed to those of regulation or custom or taste.

It is worth reiterating, too, that Business ethics applies ordinary ethical standards *in*, not *to* business situations. Life, as St Augustine said, is not a spectacle but a predicament. In real-life business situations, we are *in* the predicament, we are faced with a problem which is practical not abstract: not 'Is *advertising*, in itself, dishonest?' but 'Is this campaign, here and now, dishonest? And what does this mean for *my* business?'

WHAT ARE THE ETHICAL ISSUES?

To begin with, let us identify the issues which are not ethical. Issues of law or regulation are not, *per se*, ethical issues. If the exciting new campaign presented by the advertising agency uses material which has already been proscribed by the courts as 'liable to deprave or corrupt' or as 'racially inflammatory', there is no point in long discussions about the *ethics* of such a campaign. It is simply *illegal* in its present form and, as we have said before, since there is a presumption that business will obey the law, it will probably not be pursued.

Again, the regulations of the Advertising Standards Authority (ASA) apply to all advertisements in Britain. Campaign material is expected, by this code, to be, *inter alia*, legal, decent and truthful. When the Italian multinational clothes firm, Benetton, displayed posters of a newly born baby, complete with umbilical

cord and smeared with blood, there was an outcry from members
of the general public. The ASA claimed that 'Benetton has
displayed a conspicuous disregard for the sensitivities of the
public', was therefore in contravention of the ASA code and went
on, in effect, to ban the poster in Britain.[1] Benetton complied
with the ASA's demand and withdrew the poster. Although
interpretations of exactly what is decent or truthful may differ
somewhat, the expectation will be that the regulation will be
obeyed and, again, the question at issue is likely to be one of
the interpretation of facts, but it is not one of ethics.

Advertisements frequently engender fierce debate about their
propriety. Questions of taste, however, like questions of law or
regulation, should not be confused with ethical issues. In the
Benetton case mentioned above, many consumers were clearly
shocked by the intimacy and immediacy of the baby poster,
which was no doubt the intention of the business, which has
built a reputation for shock campaigns – including ones of a
black woman breastfeeding a white baby, a young nun kissing
a young priest and a campaign, eventually dropped by the
company, showing photographs of unrolled coloured condoms.[2]

Many people, on the other hand, have found such campaigns
acceptable and even exciting – as illustrated by the fact that
the breastfeeding poster won industry awards in five European
countries.[3]

Benetton, which has a turnover well in excess of £1 billion,
spent £26.6 million on advertising in 1991–2 and believes that
its advertising campaigns transcend national boundaries and are
aimed at global corporate communication. In such situations,
businesses have clearly to make choices about their marketing
strategy and views about public taste must form part of that
decision. No company wants to antagonise customers or tarnish
its own reputation. But calculations about taste are not the same
as questions about ethical status; to be in questionable or even
bad taste is not, of itself, to be unethical.

Again, the advertising and marketing of antisocial products,
such as tobacco, is something many people find morally unaccept-

---

[1] Report in *The Independent*, 4 September 1991.
[2] Fashion firm with a flair for hard sell, *The Independent*, 5 September 1991.
[3] Fashion firm, *The Independent*.

able. However, society does not forbid the smoking of cigarettes or their advertisement, and we cannot insist that business make our moral choices for us. While there is a market, there will be provision and where there is legal provision, there will be marketing of the product. Cigarette advertising is heavily circumscribed in Britain, most of the rest of Europe and America; it is not allowed on television in many countries and health warnings must be prominently displayed on packets. Within these parameters, however, it is legal. There may be a business ethics issue here about product safety and there is no doubt a personal ethics issue for the employees of tobacco firms, but it is something of a red herring to see the concern as primarily one of marketing or advertising.

What, then are the genuine ethical issues raised by marketing and advertising policies? How might advertising be seen to contravene the principles of justice and common decency, for example? There are at least two notions commonly assumed to indicate the moral uncertainty of advertising: they are its *manipulativeness* and its *untruthfulness*. Let me take these one by one.

ADVERTISING AS MANIPULATIVE

The relationship between business and its customers is, within classical capitalism, bounded only by the market. Business is there to make profits by selling to the consumer but it will only be able to do so if its offering is what the consumer wants. The 'invisible hand' of the market mechanism will protect both producer and consumer: the former can get as high a price for his goods or services as the market will bear and the latter will be protected by market forces from unacceptable goods and unreasonable prices. But such a satisfactory situation can only be achieved if there is a free market in information too; if the customer has enough accurate information to be able to make rational decisions between products. It also requires that the customer is able to choose freely what to buy and what not to. I will return to the need for accurate information when I go on to look at the possible *untruthfulness* of advertising. For the moment, I want to look at the notion of free choice and how this may be inhibited by marketing manipulation.

Advertising does not just inform, it also, and perhaps more importantly, persuades. It does not only let consumers know what is available, it extols the claimed virtues of this or that brand, exhorting the customer to choose one rather than another. And, it is argued by some commentators, it not only encourages people to satisfy their wants, in effect, it *creates* these wants. Consumers did not simply wake up one morning demanding stripes in their toothpaste, rather, the stripes were the latest marketing ploy in a mature toothpaste market in which manufacturers then went out to create the *need* for their product. This is the argument of the American economist John Kenneth Galbraith, who dubbed it 'the dependence effect'. Consumers, he argues, are the pawns of the advertisers, who manufacture not only their products but the demand for their products.[4] The connection, Galbraith goes on, between production and wants is marketing – advertising and salesmanship. It is not possible to think of human wants as independently determined when it is clear that the function of advertising is exactly to create these wants – to tell people that they cannot live without things of which they previously had no knowledge. The moral basis of free market economics, then, which depends on freedom of choice by the consumer to determine what he or she really wants, is thus undermined. Rather than the market serving consumers, they are merely used by it.

But is it really the case that advertising need be manipulative in the way in which this argument suggests? Talk about needs and wants takes us back to basic human requirements for the sustenance of life itself. Of course it is true that we do not *need* stripes in our toothpaste; even the lack of toothpaste without stripes is unlikely to be life-threatening. Ultimately, the needs which arise spontaneously in the individual are limited almost only to food, shelter and sex. Anything beyond this is culturally induced; so far, Galbraith is right. But it is surely exactly beyond this basic level that the requirements of civilised life begin to be felt; almost all our wants are, in this sense, socially developed: not only our desire for a Walkman but our need for music itself. If human beings are indeed the victims of a 'dependence effect', it is at a much more basic level than Galbraith's analysis allows;

[4] J. K. Galbraith, *The Affluent Society*, Houghton Mifflin, 1967.

it is at the level of social and cultural life itself. Advertising, seen in this context, is no more 'manipulative' than any other form of social intercourse; it modifies and shapes, as do many other things, our view of the world, our notions about the quality of life. This is not to say that advertising may not *in fact* sometimes be manipulative by being self-consciously untruthful, but is it, by its very nature, untruthful?

ADVERTISING AS UNTRUTHFUL

The claim that advertising is untruthful and that salespeople systematically misrepresent reality is often the crux of most consumers' reservations about ethical probity here. Advertising makes unjustifiable claims for its products; it distorts the truth and presents the world in its own terms, for its own ends. Eating a certain kind of ice-cream does not really make you more attractive to the opposite sex any more than brand X shampoo will guarantee you hair like the model – never mind his Armani suit and Mercedes sports car. Certain claims are illegal or against regulation, which is why a well-known lager styles itself modestly as only 'probably' the best! But, in general, advertisements are not intended to present the literal, or exhaustive or scientific truth.

The whole issue of what constitutes 'truth' or 'reality' is, of course, a complex one. It is not simply to make excuses for those who seek to persuade us to buy their wares, to make the point again that the *context* and *purpose* of a claim is significant here. And it is not to become too anarchically relativistic to acknowledge that reality is many-faceted: it is not an absolute, a 'thing', description of which is single and simple. Again, information is seldom, if ever, neutral; it has to be presented and received, and how this is done will inevitably depend on the position of the presenter and the expectations of the perceiver. This is as true for scientists and historians, say, as it is for advertising executives. Scientists present their facts in the context of their theoretical understanding of the world they seek to understand and explain. A mere presentation of 'facts', on their own, without selection or emphasis, would not constitute any kind of an explanation, even if it were possible.[5] A historian does not simply present 'facts' either, but seeks to use the facts to give an account of a constructed past reality. Which facts are relevant, which are emphasised or played down, will largely depend on the aim and interpretation of the scholar. As the historian of ideas John Passmore puts it,

> Nothing is more irritating to the botanist or the geologist than the presumption that every flower or every stone is of equal interest to him. A physicist is interested only in such physical operations as bear upon a problem he is investigating; a historian, similarly, will refer only to those facts which in some way bear upon the story he is telling.[6]

And what is the case for science and history, which we often think of as being 'objectively' true, is even more clearly so for poetry or, dare one say it, advertising. In both of these cases, the avowed intention is to move us, to reach our emotions, to change our perceptions and even our attitudes. We do not ask of poetry whether it is literally true. Is Shakespeare sure of his facts when he tells us 'How sharper than a serpent's tooth it is to have a thankless child?' Indeed, do serpents have teeth? And if they do, has he personally experienced their sharpness? Even if he has, how can one make a comparison between physical and emotional pain, and if one could, how can he presume that his pain comparisons are the same as my pain comparisons and your pain comparisons ... ? It is clear that the man was not telling the truth. We do not normally subject Shakespeare to this kind of inquisition because we are aware of what he is trying to do: not to give us factual information about pain thresholds, but to inspire us with a certain emotional response to a central experience of the human condition.

Advertisements, too, in their own way, aspire to create a response, to seduce us, to persuade us to a point of view and if they use symbol and hyperbole to do so, we surely cannot claim to be unaware of this or insist on taking it entirely literally. This may all sound dangerously relativistic, a licence to peddle any

[5] See S. B. Banes, On the reception of scientific beliefs, in B. Barnes, (ed.) *The Sociology of Science*, Penguin, 1972, p. 269.
[6] John Passmore, *The objectivity of history*, in Patrick Gardiner, (ed.), *The Philosophy of History*, Oxford University Press, 1974, pp. 151–2.

lies and distortions whatever, but, of course, it is not. The recognition that reality has to be created in most instances does not mean that it can be made up in any way whatsoever. Science is not the same as science fiction; a historical account is not an historical novel; we can and do appreciate the difference between Carlyle on the French Revolution and *A Tale of Two Cities*, without having to insist that only one of them is 'true'. And as far as advertising is concerned, even Galbraith agrees that modern audiences, weaned on the extravagances of television commercials and glossy magazine ads, apply an automatic discount rate to advertising's claims.[7]

But the point here is not to produce an apology for advertising or to excuse or disregard its more than occasional crudeness, vulgarity and disingenuousness. It is rather to emphasise the importance of the social context in terms of which all information about the world is given and received, so that a responsible and ethical framework can be developed for business. But before I try to develop such a framework, let me look briefly at another aspect of marketing practice – business's marketing of itself in its development of its corporate communications and corporate identity.

PR – MANIPULATIVE AND UNTRUE?

Public Relations used to get a very bad press. It was thought to employ the methods of propaganda to confuse the public with half-truths and downright lies in order to present the murky dealings of large companies as open, honest and fair. In more recent times, corporate communications and corporate identity, the new names for largely the same enterprise, have managed to present themselves as more professional, scientific and acceptable. The changes are probably skin-deep, but this does not mean that the activities are necessarily unethical. Indeed, for a business to fail to present an acceptable identity, both internally and externally, is to be remiss in the pursuit of the business aim. Long-term owner value can, these days, probably only be secured if a business is very self-conscious about the way it talks, and listens, to stakeholders inside and outside the enterprise.

---

[7] Galbraith, *Affluent Society*, p. 325.

Does this presentation of the best possible image for the company necessarily involve economy with the truth? As in the case of product advertising, marketing the company itself surely involves creating a reality, which, on the face of it, scarcely sounds honest. Yet the most successful Corporate Communications will create an identity which is not plucked out of the air but closely demarcated by a track record. To try to sell the wrong reality or the chief executive's desired reality is almost certain to be unsuccessful and counter-productive.

This is why the Corporate Communications professionals prefer the term 'identity' to that of 'image', the latter suggesting merely the packaging of a business in an acceptable and attractive way. Identity, on the other hand, according to Wally Olins, one of the industry's gurus, cannot simply be a slogan, a mere collection of phrases; it must be visible, tangible and all-embracing. Everything that the organisation does must be an affirmation of its identity.[8] But why does identity need to be created at all? Isn't the point here that it is unethical to use shareholder funds simply to follow a fashion or a management whim which makes no contribution to long-term owner value? If you are a successful, exciting business at the cutting edge of your industry, full of enthusiasm and plans for the future, surely you do not need to tell people that, far less spend large amounts of money creating a persona with which your employees and shareholders will empathise? Yet the experience of many large and successful organisations seems to suggest otherwise. For example, Sir Denys Henderson was surprised to discover, when he took over as Chairman of ICI, that, in spite of the company's profitability and its research record, people thought it was boring; and not only people outside the business but employees too were unclear about its direction and strategy.[9] An update of its identity was developed along with a worldwide advertising campaign which considerably increased awareness at home, and overseas, where 60% of the business's assets were. Again, Hanson's corporate advertising campaign turned it from a successful but little known conglomerate into a household name and is estimated to have increased its market capitalisation by some £1.4 billion.[10]

[8] Wally Olins, *Corporate Identity*, Thames and Hudson, 1989, p. 7.
[9] Corporate eyes, ears and mouths, *The Economist*, 18 March 1989, p. 105.
[10] ibid. Corporate eyes, *The Economist*.

If a clear Corporate Identity generally increases understanding of the business by its customers and shareholders, what does it do for its employees? The logos, colours, names, symbols which distinguish the organisation, says Wally Olins, 'serve the same purpose as religious symbolism, chivalric heraldry or national flags . . . they encapsulate and make vivid a collective sense of belonging and purpose'.[11] Are we back to manipulation here on another level? Ought Corporate Communication to be used to get everybody in the business marching in the same direction? Clearly, again it will depend on how it is used. Since the 1974 Employment Protection Act, companies are statutorily bound to give employees certain kinds of information (for example, financial results). Management, then, has a legal duty to communicate with staff and ethically this should aim to inform and not to conceal: as has sometimes been suggested, 'Clarity begins at home.'[12]

Particularly in situations of rapid corporate change, the corporate 'reality' may have to be pretty well constantly identified and articulated, particularly for those within the business. This is not only a matter of mapping the strategy so that people's performance will be better as a result of knowing where they are going: it is also a requirement of the ethical treatment of employees as people. If the aim of Corporate Communication is not to communicate but to deceive, to pedal a 'reality' which is at variance with what people perceive to be the logic of their situation, the results, as with blatantly contrafactual advertising, will be counter-productive. As Orwell, that great decrier of 'doublespeak' said, 'The great enemy of clear language is insincerity. When there is a gap between one's real and one's declared aims, one turns . . . to long words and exhausted idioms, like a cuttlefish squirting out ink.'[13]

THE ETHICAL CONTEXT OF ADVERTISING AND
SALESMANSHIP

We have already raised some of the questions of the Ethical Decision Model in the general area of advertising and marketing –

[11] Olins, *Corporate Identity* p. 9.
[12] D. Bernstein, *Company Image and Reality*, Holt Rinehart, 1984, p. 233.
[13] George Orwell, *Shooting an Elephant and Other Essays*, Secker and Warburg, 1950.

identifying what the ethical questions at issue actually are, for example. ('Is advertising unethical?' is probably not, as it stands, a very sensible question.) We have also emphasised the particularity of the issue as it affects *this* business at *this* time and the importance of identifying the external constraints, such as the law or regulation, which may make the question one of legality or compliance rather than morality.

Further, we have identified the ethical concerns as being about the perceived untruthfulness and manipulativeness of advertising and marketing. But we have also argued that 'absolute' truth is a chimera, and that 'reality' is socially constructed according to which story you are telling. This may seem a dangerously relativistic line to take and one which scarcely allows us to make judgements about truthfulness, for example. Yet we do know what is true or false – but only in a context. We do not expect, or get, detailed, objective consumer advice from a salesperson; for that, we would expect to go to a consumer association. Salespeople who do not spend as much time extolling a rival product as they do their own brand are not lying but merely doing their job. On the other hand, lying is no part of that job. If asked specifically about the expenses of maintenance or whether the projected motorway will come past the end of the garden, making the sale does not take precedence over telling the truth. What, then, should be the ethical context of advertising and salesmanship? In the general terms of the Ethical Decision Model, activity should be assessed in terms of the aim of the business, that is, the effect on long-term owner value, in the context of justice and ordinary decency. From the point of view of long-term owner value, it is clearly important that any sale made should be satisfactory to both buyer and seller. This implies that information must be sought and given so that rational choices can be made. What do justice and decency suggest here? Let us try to be rather more specific about how this might work out in the advertising or marketing context:

- appropriateness: it is important that both parties, buyer and seller, understand the social framework of sales and act appropriately in the circumstances. The buyer should not be expecting objective consumer advice and the seller should not believe that telling lies is all right provided that a sale is made.

- relevance: if a rational transaction is to be entered into, it is important that relevant information is not withheld. Some information (for example, safety standards) may be relevant to any potential buyer; some may only be important to a particular buyer (whether the house is within easy distance of good schools is probably important information for parents of young children but not for a retired couple).
- respect – of both parties for each other: respect for the buyer and for his or her right to information relevant to the transaction, respect for the professionalism of the seller whose aim should not be to *deceive* but to *persuade.*
- non-compulsion: choices should not be limited artificially, or sales compelled, for example, by involving customers in a sales situation without their being aware of it as such. Sales pitches which begin by purporting to be 'surveys' may limit customer choice unacceptably, as people are not aware (and are not encouraged to be aware) that they are operating in a buyer/seller context.

These conditions may never all be entirely fulfilled in any particular sales activity but they provide some useful reference points by which to judge specific transactions.

The ethical enterprise will be self-conscious about such issues and seek to incorporate them in its systems and structures. It will:

- make such conditions central in the training of its sales and marketing people, making it clear, for example, that persuasion is not the same as either deceit or compulsion;
- support the rights of consumers to access to accurate information on products, prices etc.;
- emphasise consumer freedom of choice by giving adequate time for the buyer to reflect and reject a sale.

In the case of advertising, not all the conditions apply directly, but appropriateness and respect may be much to the point. Advertising may be about creating a 'reality' but not just any reality. Presenting the product in the best possible light is one thing; lies are quite another. Again, legitimate persuasion must be bounded by respect for the consumer and other stakeholders. In the case of the Benetton baby advertisement, it was less the picture of the newborn child that offended many people than the use of such a potent and emotive image for such a purpose and that the main aim of the image was simply to shock. Many people felt that it was unethical to exploit the miracle of birth to sell sweaters.[14]

The use of sex to sell products is regarded with deep distaste by many people and although, as we have pointed out, the tasteless is not necessarily the same as the unethical, there are cases when the exploitation of certain groups – notably women – would seem to be unacceptable in moral terms. Sex-based advertisements hardly exemplify ordinary decency in the treatment of half the population. In addition, they may actually be counter-productive since research has shown that three out of four women and three out of five men object to the exploitation of sex in advertising.[15] To risk offending such a high proportion of stakeholders is probably not good strategy anyway and a carefully developed corporate identity may be badly damaged by a campaign which is seen as unjust (exploitative) and lacking in ordinary decency.

In the case of marketing, although the appropriateness criterion would suggest that a certain caution in the face of manufacturers' claims is in order, in some cases the apparent objectivity of the claims may be misleading. Food labelling is often in this category. Claims that products are 'made from natural ingredients', organic, 'low fat' or 'sugar free' are common but *have no legal definition*. Government guidelines exist in Britain on when a product can claim these things but they are voluntary and frequently ignored by manufacturers and marketeers.[16] The fact that consumers frequently buy such foods out of concern for their own health and that of their families may compound the felony and offend against the non-compulsion criterion. Choice is artificially limited by the strong suggestion that not to buy the 'healthy' (and frequently more expensive) product is to be less responsible than one might be as, say, a wife or mother.

The appropriateness criterion has already been alluded to for sales. Telling 'the truth, the whole truth and nothing but the

---

[14] Should this ad be banned? *Evening Standard*, 4 September 1991.

[15] Report by the Advertising Standards Authority, see No to the sexy sell, *Sunday Times*, 11 February 1990.

[16] Health claims on food baffle the shopper, *The Times*, 12 November 1991. From October 1993, manufacturers are obliged, when making a nutritional claim, to give full nutritional details on the label.

truth' is probably only to be appropriately demanded in a court of law. Again, however, relevant information needs to be given so that consumers can make rational choices. What about the relevance of lines like, 'Madam looks wonderful in that hat', or 'The outfit is so slimming'? Are they appropriate? They may not be entirely factual but whether they are deceitful rather than persuasive will depend on the situation in which they are used. People don't only buy products; they also buy dreams and the 'feel-good' factor may be as much a part of their 'rational decision' to purchase as the colour or the quality or the price. Products are often chosen, perfectly reasonably and self-consciously, for all these reasons. Someone who was well aware of the combination of factors involved here was Charles Revson of Revlon Inc., who claimed, 'In the factory we make cosmetics; in the store we sell hope.'[17]

There is a fine line, in some cases, between selling 'hope' and making false claims. A particular face cream may make me feel more attractive but am I misled or simply gullible if I believe that it will make me look twenty years younger? If I buy the cream because it makes me feel good, I cannot claim to have been misled if it does no more than that. If I buy it because I have been assured that it will get rid of my wrinkles and it does not, I have not been given the information to allow me to make a rational choice. The sales pitch is not only hyperbolic, which I might expect, but false and therefore, by definition, unethical.

DOES MARKETING CONTRIBUTE TO LONG-TERM OWNER VALUE?

This might seem to be a question of fact rather than one of ethical importance. But if the answer is no, then the managers who spend collectively billions a year on promoting their products are every bit as guilty of theft from the shareholder as those who might spend money on buying themselves yachts or villas in the South of France. If they cannot show that any of these things contribute to long-term owner value, they should be spending the money on projects or policies which do, or reinvesting

[17] Quoted in Theodore Levitt, The morality(?) of advertising, *Harvard Business Review*, July 1970.

it in the company in some other way, or distributing it as dividend.

There is some evidence to suggest that the sales impact of advertising may not be all it is assumed to be. When Mike Mile took over as president of Kraft Foods in 1990, he inherited a turnover of some $23 billion and a $1.2 billion advertising budget. After studying the figures, however, he found no correlation between advertising spending and sales. He experimented by doubling the budgets in some areas and found it made no difference; he cut budgets by half in other areas and found no difference. Even when he stopped advertising in some places altogether, it apparently made no difference.[18]

This was, of course, a rather subjective and limited experiment and its conclusions could hardly be described as scientific. But recent academic research on marketing promotions has also suggested that they do not have the expected results. Research recently carried out by the London Business School, for example, found that consumer promotions for established brands of grocery products are not brand-building, although they account for about a quarter of all marketing expenditure.[19]

Apart from such evidence, however, there has been little detailed research in this area and the belief of large, successful businesses is often that they remain large and successful in part because of their marketing strategy. This may be largely an article of faith but is nonetheless strongly held. If it were shown conclusively in the future that marketing was ineffectual or that advertising was merely an amusing diversion which had little influence on consumer choice, the real ethical question for business could move from the honesty and acceptability of marketing tactics to the justification of an outlay for no added value.

A POSTSCRIPT ON SPONSORSHIP

The Royal Shakespeare Company's 1993 production of *Hamlet* was sponsored by Persil soap powder and Flora margarine. BT funds the Monteverdi Choir and Northern Ballet and American

[18] The adman's lament, *The Guardian*, 21 September 1992.
[19] The After Effects of Consumer Promotions, Preliminary Report, London Business School, 1991.

Express is the money behind the Brighton Festival. All seem happy; all believe they gain; the arts from the money to which they would not otherwise have access and the companies from association with artistic achievement and the public polishing of their corporate image. The theatre companies, orchestras, exhibitions and festivals which are supported are thereby enabled to do what they would not otherwise have been able to afford and the commercial concerns get their logos prominently displayed and a chance to do some corporate entertaining.

Are there really any ethical issues involved here? Aristotle perhaps alerts us to the fundamental problem for business when he says: 'To give away money is an easy matter and in any man's power, but to decide to whom to give it and when and for what purpose and how, is neither in every man's power nor an easy matter. Hence it is that such excellence is rare and praiseworthy and noble.'[20] Recalling the business aim of the production of long-term owner value, the justification for arts and other sponsorship must be in line with this. It is not just a matter of giving away money, because the board support the Arts, but crucial, as Aristotle reminds us, 'to decide to whom to give it and when and for what purpose and how'. This can be no easy matter. It is often not clear what the direct benefits of such expenditure are in terms of the business aim.

There are also related issues of ethical significance which might be characterised as undue influence, dependence and whim. To take these one by one: there is the worry that companies which are putting large amounts of money into productions will demand a say in the production itself, not necessarily in the detail of the piece but in the choice of what is presented. American Express funded the production of a theatre company at the Brighton Festival in 1992. They were apparently delighted with the results but for the 1993 season were seeking something 'fun, new, original, general enough to please colleagues . . . and gilt edge, non-risk'.[21] Does this offend against the criterion of noncompulsion outlined above? A business may believe that it gets its money's worth out of a sponsorship but if it is the only source

---

[20] Quoted in Michael Norton, *The Corporate Donor's Handbook*, Bath Press, 1987, p. 1.
[21] Business and the Arts, Radio 4, 7 December 1992.

of finance for an artistic concern is it liable to exert undue influence on the *artistic* decisions of that concern?

For some people in the Arts, however, the real ethical issue is not possible artistic pressure but the reality that they may become very largely financially dependent on business for funding. John Nixon of the English National Opera (ENO) says, 'Sponsorship is not the icing on the cake – increasingly, it is the cake.' In 1991–2, the ENO was kept out of deficit by its sponsorship funding. The real danger here is not that of the manipulation of artistic taste or the limitation of artistic choice, it is the dreadful possibility that business will withdraw its support. As Michael Billington of *The Guardian* suggests, the Arts may be coming to rely on sponsorship for *core* funding. Business may be beginning to take over the burden of government responsibility. But, as we have argued before, business is not government and if this role may be an unintended consequence of sponsorship, business must be all the more aware of its own aim in order to avoid it.

There is also the concern that business sponsorship, not informed by the business aim, may be arbitrary. If it is no longer decided on the basis of what used to be slightingly referred to as the current enthusiasm of the Chairman's wife (the assumption being, presumably, that almost all women were more interested in the Arts than the philistine captains of industry), it is still the personal interests of board members which decide where the money goes. BP cut its Arts budget of £1.3 million when its Chairman, Robert Horton, a great supporter of the Arts, resigned. It is quite likely that Horton, with his tough business mind, made his decisions in this area on business criteria, rather than on personal artistic preferences, but the new board decided otherwise. Most large companies now have a committee of the board, armed with specific criteria related to the business aim, in terms of which they decide the corporate giving of the company and this begins to address the worry, from the point of view of both business and the Arts, that sponsorship is in any sense a matter of whim.

Business's support for the Arts is not unethical, but it can raise a number of ethical dilemmas for business itself. These are best dealt with initially by those in the business keeping always in mind the business aim, and thereafter working within terms of the criteria of appropriateness, relevance, respect and non-compulsion. Such an approach will allow business to create long-term owner value within the context of ethical priorities.

7

The environment

Why should I care about posterity? What's posterity ever done for me?

(Groucho Marx)

Business is often seen as the enemy of the environment . . . There is, however, a tide of change and it is now increasingly being seen as the essential partner, as part of the solution and not the problem.

(Peter Bright, Shell International Petroleum Co Ltd)

Quite suddenly, or so it seemed, in the 1980s people became concerned about the planet. Of course, there had always been those who preached the gospel of environmentalism but they were relatively few and it was believed that most sported sandals and long hair. Then the hole in the ozone layer was discovered and the green movement entered a new phase. In the past, dirty air or water had been seen as lamentable but largely containable; there was always the possibility of finding an unpolluted part of the world in which to start again and, if we thought it was worth the money, we could always clean up our own back yard.

But a hole in the stratospheric ozone layer which could allow harmful ultra-violet radiation to reach the earth's surface seemed irrecoverable and to threaten us all. The problem was perceived to be global and within a few years an international agreement was signed to limit CFC emissions and the Commission of the European Community had brought in over 250 environmental directives, mostly aimed at businesses.

At the same time, business itself became aware of the market for green products. The green consumer was king and there were premium prices to be won for 'ozone-friendly' deodorant spray and fridges free of CFCs. Thus, in a number of ways, business, in pursuing its aim, has been brought up against the demands of the environmental lobby and has had to make decisions which reflect its ethical position here. This is important as a business environmental strategy and practice is often critical to its success – by influencing everything from who will want to work for the company to whether it gets planning permission for its new factory.

If business's perception of the importance of environmentalists and environmentalism has had to change, Peter Bright's comment quoted above also identifies a change in the attitude of most conservationists both to business and to their own campaign priorities. In the 1970s and early 1980s, Greens were less focused, less organised, still marginal as an interest group and dismissable as something of a lunatic fringe by much of the business community. In turn, Greens themselves were more extreme in their responses to business: many of them opposed its central values, the profit motive and the market mechanism, claiming that these were inimical to the protection of the environment. These so-called 'deep ecologists' or 'Dark Greens' still exist but they are only one part of the Green movement, much of which is now concerned not with 'zero growth' but with 'sustainability', and in this latter context business is seen as having a central, and positive, role to play. I shall return later to the problems with which this changed perception faces business. As I shall argue, however, in spite of the growing importance of the environment for business policy, environmentalism as such poses a quite limited number of specifically ethical issues for business.

WHY SHOULD BUSINESS BE GREEN?

Is it the lot of business to add to its own costs by being greener? If the aim of business is to secure long-term owner value, is it ethical to spend shareholders' money on cleaning air or decontaminating rivers? The answer is, it depends on your business; but it is likely that almost all businesses will contribute somehow and in some way to pollution, if not by emissions into earth or sea or sky, then by making the environment noisier or dirtier or by using energy in an inefficient way. It is the argument of this chapter that it is part of the business ethics problem to identify the proper response of businesses to the potentially infinite demands of environmentalists.

It is often assumed nowadays that business has an obligation to be environmentally responsible. But what is the basis of this obligation? Do people (including people in the future) have a *right* to a clean environment? The question of the meaningfulness of abstract moral rights is one about which philosophers argue; it is also one which need not detain us. For the basis of business's obligation here is not abstract but bounded, as always in our argument, by the aims of business itself and, in the particular case, by the aims of *this* business. It is not a question of business in general having an obligation to save the earth from fatal exploitation but much more a matter of seeing particular environmental issues in the contexts within which they occur. The response of the ethical business to the challenge of the environment cannot, and should not, be a promise to halt global warming or replant the rainforests. Rather, an acceptance of the importance for the business of protecting the environment will make the ethical organisation take a long hard look at its own structures and processes to see where it may be polluting in ways which it can eliminate or mitigate.

There are many reasons, both positive and negative, why business is becoming environmentally aware. It is recognised, for example, that good environmental management can improve employee morale and help attract better quality staff (especially among young people, with whom environmental policy ranks high on any list of priorities for business); cut costs by eliminating waste and saving energy; and bring competitive advantage by putting the company at the forefront of technical and regulatory development.

Failure to be environmentally responsible, on the other hand, can be very counter-productive, leading to fines for non-compliance with increasingly tough environmental regulations; to loss of profits, loss of good staff and loss of reputation.

Increasingly too, businesses will demand high environmental standards from their suppliers, and investors from the companies they support. To fail to reach these standards will mean loss of business and ultimately, perhaps, business failure.

None of these reasons is specifically ethical and most of the environmental decisions taken by businesses will be justified in just such terms. This is not, of course, to say that they are in any way unethical and most businesses will, in addition to such commercial considerations, be gratified that they are doing the right thing.

HOW SHOULD BUSINESS PROCEED HERE?

As we suggested in our framework (part I), in dealing with such complex issues a business needs to keep its head and set about identifying what is actually at stake. This is not the same as committing itself with an abstract moral fervour to saving the planet but rather involves looking at identifiable environmental problems for *this* business at *this* time. We need, to begin with, to separate out the background questions of environmental *interest* from the business ethics questions in this particular case. We need, in other words, to find out what exactly *is* the question at issue in each particular case.

We also need to say something of what we mean by 'pollution'. *The Shorter Oxford Dictionary* is quite precise here: to pollute something is 'to make [it] physically impure, foul or filthy'. This suggests a rather limited notion of environmental pollution as rendering air or water physically impure etc. which would imply that the environment was a business concern largely of manufacturing industry. But the term has acquired much wider connotations in common usage, going beyond physical effluents to noise, packaging and even design and signage, all of which are claimed to have an impact on the environment.[1] Although this widening of the concept might also seem both to dilute its impact and to involve business in yet wider issues of social and public policy, if these are perceived as relevant by shareholders, customers and employees, the business clearly has an incentive at least to consider what its policy in relation to them should be. What is relevant here is not a precise definition of a term but, as ever, a precise understanding on the part of the business of its own aims and ends.

IS BUSINESS ITSELF THE ETHICAL PROBLEM?

The answer is no. Just as we are not looking in this book to justify the bases of ethics, neither are we looking to justify the

[1] We even hear now of 'colour pollution'. See Goodbye to grey, *Financial Times*, 12 June 1991, p. 11.

existence of business. Business creates wealth; it can also create environmental problems. But the question of whether business should exist at all because it creates environmental damage is not the business ethics issue. As we shall see, it is no longer the issue for much of the Green movement either, which is increasingly much more interested in asking instead what business can and should do to mitigate pollution and waste.

The 'Dark Greens' were, and still are, anti-business. They oppose growth and advocate the maintenance of the status quo as a way of ensuring that what are seen as the excesses of the market economy are limited. Only thus, they argue, can an acceptable quality of human life be protected. For them, business itself, its methods and profit-driven attitudes, are the central problem. But the argument has increasingly been made that their case is radically flawed both theoretically and practically. Theoretically, in that it suggests that the quality of the environment is the supreme human value and the one to which all others should be subject. This is, of course, at least contestable; one might argue, for example, that liberty or equality are human values every bit as important as – or more so than – clean air or the protection of the rainforest. If the attainment of a clean environment were only made possible by, for example, a serious limitation of liberty or the establishment of conditions of gross inequality, at least some people would want to say that it would not be worth the achievement.

Again, as more pragmatic Greens argue, zero growth is hardly even an option. The population of the world is expected to rise by more than a billion in the 1990s and this will inevitably drive growth. And even if no growth were possible, this would simply leave us in a position where business had nothing to spend on environmental improvement. Better, argue these people, to influence business thinking in this area and solicit its support, than to cry in the wilderness for no growth.

As the Green lobby has become more sophisticated, it has increasingly realised that hard choices have often to be made between its own projects. Resources here, as in other areas of the economy, are limited and, once spent on limiting air pollution, for example, are not available for cutting down on effluent. Whereas the original Greens tended to demand everything, and immediately, much of the argument now revolves around which trade-offs will achieve the greatest overall impact on the environment. The 'Dark Greens' were unable to compromise; they demanded clean air and they meant 100 per cent clean air. This was an article of faith and not a negotiating point. But the realisation that there are real opportunity costs at work here has concentrated the minds of many conservationists. One American study, for example, revealed that the cost of eliminating 90 per cent of the pollutants generated in carbon steel production was 26 cents per kilo, of removing 97 per cent was $4.98 and of getting rid of 99 per cent was $32.20.[2] A law of diminishing returns may operate with many environmental issues and the Green lobby has become increasingly concerned to calculate what seems to be the best use of the available resources.

This change in Green thinking has meant that business, and certainly big business, rather than always being seen as the bogeyman, is now often depicted as the ally of the Greens. As Peter Bright says, business is less the problem than an important part of the solution. But this changed status brings its own difficulties: how, for example, is the ethical business, having recognised the importance of the environmental claim for its own operation, to decide on environmental priorities which are theoretically infinite and potentially seriously erosive of profits?

If the aim of business is to secure long-term owner value, how can a business's environmental policy (or non-policy) contribute to or detract from this? The criterion is and must be the securing of the business aim and not the desire, *per se*, to save the whale or clean the air by reducing sulphur emissions. As we have seen elsewhere, the business aim cannot simply be achieved by cost-cutting or the refusal to do anything which takes up resources, if only because stakeholders, who contribute to the success of the business, may be very concerned about the business's response, in this case, to environmental issues.

WHAT THE BUSINESS ETHICS QUESTION IS NOT

There are several other complications and confusions in this area which, although not themselves business ethics questions, are

---

[2] Robert W. Lee, Conservatives consider the crushing cost of environmental extremism, in W. M. Hoffman and J. M. Moore, *Business Ethics*, McGraw-Hill, 1990, p. 483.

often widely discussed. Sometimes this discussion is necessary and justifiable so that a rational business decision can be taken but the issues raised in this context need to be clearly differentiated from the ethical ones.

– *Not business's decision?*

Everyone is concerned with the environment and the role of business here in a way in which not everybody is concerned with, say, corporate governance or fraud. While people may be content to leave business largely to make its own decisions on the latter issues, which may seem remote and complicated, almost everyone has a view on environmental protection. Again, people are concerned in different capacities – as parents and citizens, as well as employees, customers, shareholders, etc. This complicates and often confuses the arguments made. A few years ago, a television programme interviewed managers of chemical companies about discharging effluent into rivers. At the time, the levels of effluent were not illegal, and many of them thought, *as managers*, this was acceptable as it saved business resources while staying within the law. Yet, as one of them put it, as *a responsible citizen*, he was in favour of the new, tighter legislation which was being suggested.[3]

But just because everybody has a view does not mean that everybody's view is of equal value. Business cannot simply bow to public pressure; rather, it is incumbent on business itself to work out what it must do in this context to facilitate the achievement of its aim.

– *Merely public relations?*

Because this has become an issue of concern for everyone, it can be seen as a *public relations* issue pure and simple. But if this is interpreted as the mere claim to certain policies and actions, without relating them to the business's aim or following through, the result can be completely counter-productive. In 1989, for

---

[3] Quoted in Robert E. Frederick, Is business obligated to protect the environment? Business Ethics Report on Business, Ethics and the Environment, Bentley College, October 1989, p. 3.

example, Friends of the Earth, the environmental pressure group, collected examples of businesses which cynically jumped on the ecological bandwagon and presented 'Green Con Awards' to the most blatant.[4] The resulting publicity did little to enhance these businesses' long-term owner value.

– *Really a technological question?*

Because of the technical processes which have created pollution – and may be used to reduce it – people may think of this as a *technological* problem without ethical implications. But technology can often create specifically moral dilemmas (as, for example, in the area of biotechnology) which didn't exist before.

– *Really a question of facts?*

The uncertainty of the outcome of, for example, global warming and the disagreement between experts on what will happen may seem to convert the question into one of *scientific* facts. Business will have to take account of this debate but the business ethics questions are distinct from this and still have to be answered.

– *'The best things in life are free'?*

Because no price has, in the past, been put on pollution, it has not been accounted as part of the cost of production. No one has clear property rights in the environment and thus the signal to the market has been that the air, rivers and sea are free, rather than possibly priceless. Once this is recognised, there is a tendency to see the issue as an *economic* one, a matter of establishing the market price for pollution. This has proved very difficult to determine in any conclusive way; and although the exercise may be worthwhile,[5] it cannot provide the answer to the business ethics question.

---

[4] Quoted in D. Clutterbuck and D. Snow, *Working with the Community*, Weidenfeld and Nicolson, 1990, p. 10.

[5] For a well-argued and convincing account of the economic issues which face business on the environment, see F. Cairncross, *Costing the Earth*, Economist Books, 1991, *passim.*

– *Is it a question of control?*

How can pollution best be controlled? Do we need government regulation, cost controls – like a 'carbon tax' – or would tradeable permits, allowing prescribed levels of emissions to be 'sold' by cleaner to dirtier businesses be the answer? This seems to make the question a *regulatory* or *political* one. But the business ethics question is not the same as the issue of public policy.

– *The international dimension*

Many environmental issues affect the whole world. CFCs in refrigerators in China affect the common ozone layer. All the problems of international standards and cross-cultural agreement on values rear their heads again.

All of these are issues in the general environmental debate and they generate much discussion and argument but they are not the business ethics question itself, which is more specific than these and which remains: how should the ethical organisation act when its operations impinge on the environment and how, specifically, should it conduct itself in relation to potentially wasteful or damaging practices?

In spite of (and because of) these complications at the heart of the environment debate, it is important that business is clear about its own position in the debate. Business is not there to decide on the methods of making polluters pay or drawing up lists of environmental priorities. These are questions of public policy (which governments must decide) and not of business ethics. As Frances Cairncross rightly says in her book on the economics of the environment, 'It is not the job of companies to decide what values ought to be attached to natural resources and what the priorities of environmental policy ought to be, any more than it is their job to decide what share of national income should go into education or what the speed limit should be.'[6]

Similarly, business is not primarily concerned about the debate on the scientific facts. Is the hole in the ozone layer really a long-term problem or will a solution be found before we spend billions replacing CFCs? Scientists don't agree about the answers;

[6] Cairncross, *Costing the Earth*, p. 236.

causality is difficult to prove and this is not the remit of business. This does not mean, of course, that business can ignore such issues, for it operates against the background of current public concerns which affect stakeholder perceptions and support and therefore its own success or failure. At the least, therefore, business has to be seen to be acting responsibly in the light of such perceptions and concerns: only thus will it fulfil its proper aim.

How should the ethical business decide what its environmental policy should be? The major criteria should still be: does any projected action secure long-term owner value, subject to the claims of justice and common decency? The focus on long-term owner value prevents any abstract agonising about issues which, although of clear environmental significance, are not within the power of *this* business to influence and therefore have no effect on owner value. Just as there is no point in spending time thinking through the issue of bribery in international businesses if your business is running a local sweet shop, so there is probably no need to have an extensive policy on oil pollution if you run a secretarial agency. Good is done, here as elsewhere, in minute – and practical and relevant – particulars.

On the face of it, long-term owner value is apparently not served by incurring costs which may be very heavy; but it is not only owner value but *long-term* owner value which is the aim and this involves calculations about how the various stakeholders in the business will react to the environmental policy.

This is not to say that long-term owner value is always secured by simply bowing to, rather than taking account of, stakeholder pressure. A business judgement has always to be made. What if community leaders, for example, insist that the production process be made 100 per cent clean rather than the 96 per cent to which the company is working? The acid test will be whether customers are prepared to pay for the more expensive environmentally friendly product thus produced. The business must ask itself what business it's in – producing cheaper but less green or selling green at a premium? Or again, whether, in this business, there is even a choice.

How should all this affect the decisions that business will take in relation to the environment? Should business limit pollution and contribute to enhancing the environment? As I have described above, business has gone from being largely perceived as the villain in the environmental saga to the white knight which will fund a huge cleaning-up operation. In the meantime, questions are asked by business people themselves about the extent to which business can afford the investment of billions on operations which apparently have no direct benefits but only add costs.

Posed in the abstract, the question of whether business should clean up the environment is not very helpful. Which businesses are we talking about here? What steps is it being suggested business should take? There are here a huge number of issues of politics, economics, science, technology and public policy, as well as morality. If the question is to have any meaning, it must be analysed and clarified.

To begin with, we must recall the simple fact that the aim of business is not to clean up the environment but to sustain long-term owner value. It is also true that policy questions are not put to businesses in the abstract but emerge in the context of *this* business *now*. The question that a particular business needs to address, then, is likely to be specific and not necessarily ethical in nature. Thus, the relevant question for a particular business will not be whether business should clean up the environment or even whether *this* business should clean up the environment, but, for example, whether we should introduce recycling of our packaging.

In coming to a decision, the business may give consideration to any number of factors: for example, that such recycling is to become a legal requirement, making the choice not whether but when; that such a move would put the business ahead of its competitors in customer provision; or, conversely, that customers will be lost to the opposition if not; that money will, in the end, be saved by more economical packaging, and so on and so on.

All of these create or contribute to long-term owner value and may give an answer to the packaging question without recourse to any heart searching of a specifically ethical nature.

Those in the business may also, of course, want to do the *right* thing and believe that pollution, to which packaging contributes, is the *wrong* thing. If the business judgement about the action which will secure long-term owner value happily coincides with the desire to do the right thing, all well and good. Mixed motives are the stuff of life and not to be disparaged. It does not make the action any less right that it is also judged to be advantageous.

But what if the commercial judgement is that the money spent on packaging recycling will not secure long-term owner value, but recycling is still thought to be right? The short answer is that if it does not contribute to long-term owner value, it is not a possible business option. Business is not there to sacrifice its proper end to cleaning up the environment (although it is unlikely these days that it will achieve its proper end without a responsible environmental policy). The moral probity of the business is not achieved in sacrificing what are, by definition, its aims. Indeed, it would be unethical for a business to put its employees' and shareholders' interests at risk because it chose to fail to achieve its declared end.

The ethical question may then seem to become: is it less morally reprehensible to put people's jobs and investments at risk than to add to pollution? Yet this is not really even a dilemma for business whose very *raison d'être* is stakeholder interest rather than beautifying the environment. The ethical business acts so as to fulfil its aim in the context of justice and decency. This requires primarily that people are not disappointed in their reasonable expectations or cheated out of what they signed up for.

Of course, there is still scope for good deeds in business. The board may believe that recycling is a responsible and worthy policy. All well and good, so long as it enhances the corporate identity, gives the business a competitive edge, and/or attracts and retains the best staff; and only a very short-sighted business would be unaware of the importance these days of a responsible environmental policy.

What about the ethical values of justice and common decency

which we have identified as those which constrain the ethical organisation? How, for example, should the business deal with the requirement to be honest in relation to its environmental record? Should a business disclose everything about, say, its manufacturing processes, including every detail of its waste disposal? Again, the question hardly makes sense in the abstract. Waste disposal after the manufacture of lemonade is clearly rather different from that in the production of nuclear power. Significant problems only arise when we identify questions in a specific business at a specific time.

Take the case, then, of a manufacturing business selling a factory on land which has buried on it some low-grade toxic waste. Does the seller have a duty to give details to any prospective buyer? The answer is not entirely clear-cut.

The business's aim is to sell the property which will contribute to long-term owner value. But to sell it in any way and by any means, however dishonest, is unlikely to achieve this end. If it becomes known, for example, that the purchaser has been lied to or blatantly misled, this may reflect on the seller, not just in future property transactions, but across the whole enterprise which is now branded as untrustworthy. 'My word is my bond' is still an important basic business principle.

What if the business involved were not a manufacturing but a property business, an estate agency, for example? Total disclosure might seem essential in this case if repeat business were to be expected. On the other hand, estate agents are known to be often rather poetic, even fanciful, in describing their properties, as almost any hopeful viewer of a 'des. res.' finds out. In this case, context is important. *Caveat emptor* does not in any way excuse lying or cheating, but what it does do is focus attention on the two-way conversation that such transactions are expected to involve. The prospective buyer may have to ask before he gets all the information he requires. The seller is there to sell, not necessarily at any price or by any means whatever, but he is probably not, in his business, going to be quick to mention the possible drawbacks of the property or the better alternative on offer from his competitor. As we have pointed out elsewhere, 'the truth, the whole truth, and nothing but the truth' is a requirement in a court of law; outside that context, however, it may have little meaning. Not only in business but in everyday life one is expected to evaluate the context in order to make an appropriate response.

Does this mean, then, that the seller of polluted land has no obligation to tell the truth here, that it is purely the responsibility of the buyer to ask the right questions? Not necessarily; again, it depends on the circumstances. If the seller is asked outright about buried waste, it is simply right to tell the truth. Business may not depend on the truth, the whole truth, etc., but it does depend on a presumption of no lying and cheating. But if the toxic substance is indeed low-grade and well buried, it may be irrelevant to the land use which the purchaser has in mind. In this case, disclosure for disclosure's sake may be unnecessary. If, on the other hand, the seller knows that the potential buyer is intending to build a children's playground on the site, it would be incumbent on the responsible business to disclose the facts, even if the argument were concurrently made that the waste itself was safely and properly disposed of.

Again, it is worth emphasising that such decisions will often be made on quite practical, commercial grounds without any direct reference to ethical considerations. A seller will disclose because of a legal requirement or because he calculates that the damage to his reputation if he even appears to have misled the buyer would be too grave to take that risk. On the positive side too, businesses which have been honest and gone public in situations where the truth might have seemed likely to harm their reputations have often done well out of their decision. One thinks of Johnson and Johnson's successful handling of the Tylenol poisoning scare.[7] On the other hand, Perrier, the mineral water producer, were much criticised for the inept and secretive way in which they dealt with a benzine pollution of their source. Although they withdrew millions of bottles of product from sale, they were perceived to have acted too late and under pressure and their market share fell badly as a result. In a similar way, Dow Corning, the American industrial supplies company, got into trouble by failing to respond quickly to the claim that the silicone breast implants they were selling to women worldwide were not safe. Only numerous impending lawsuits and embarrass-

---

[7] When a batch of the company's Tylenol painkillers were contaminated in 1982, Johnson and Johnson acted quickly and with great openness, winning widespread admiration.

ing public congressional investigations eventually forced the company to withdraw from the breast implant market altogether.
The cost of litigation and settlements may still sink the business
but even if it survives the blow to its finances it will still have
a long struggle to restore its credibility.[8]

GREEN IS HERE TO STAY

Business does not create society's priorities and values, yet it
contributes to their development and reinforces them. It seems
unlikely that we will ever again fail to be aware of the pollution
of the planet; as one ecological preoccupation is put to rest,
another will be addressed. Awareness of the fragility of the
ecosystem is part of the modern mindset and of the context in
which modern business operates. As such, it has to be taken
into account in attaining the business end in the honest and
responsible manner to which the ethical organisation aspires.

[8] For an account of Dow's response to the breast implant scare, see Getting the chemistry
wrong, *Financial Times*, 25 March 1992, p. 16.

8

Corporate governance

Quis custodiet ipsos custodes?   (Juvenal)

The accumulation of all powers ... in the same hands,
whether of one, a few or many, and whether hereditary,
self-appointed or elective, may justly be pronounced the very
definition of tyranny.   (James Madison, *Federalist* No. 47)

Our proposals aim to strengthen the unitary board system
and increase its effectiveness, not to replace it ... It must,
however, be recognised that no system of control can eliminate the risk of fraud without so shackling companies as to
impede their ability to compete in the market place.
                                         (The Cadbury Report)

It is not hard to see why there has been such interest recently
in so apparently unlikely a subject as corporate governance. The
scandals of the past few years, in Britain and elsewhere in the
international world of business, culminated for many people in
the Maxwell affair, where a powerful individual seemed to have
ruled a business empire virtually unchallenged and, in the process, to have ruined the lives and hopes of thousands of pensioner
stakeholders in his enterprise. In this case, the law appeared to
have been systematically broken and, while it was recognised
that no system of control can completely protect against those
prepared to ride roughshod over legal and conventional arrangements, questions were inevitably asked about the role of those
who had held positions of power in the Maxwell empire. What
about the board? Where were the other executive directors? What
were the non-executives doing? Did shareholders know anything
of what was going on? If not, why not? What were the arrangements in this business for control of the chairman? In other

words, the affair raised starkly and practically for many who had never considered them before, the central questions of corporate governance: who has power, from whom, to do what? And who makes sure it has been done?

It is not only the examples of fraud and malpractice which have concentrated people's minds on the whole issue of accountability in business. As corporations have become very large, so we have become more and more aware of their influence on all our lives. They employ very large numbers of the workforce; their effect on the implementation of public policy can be crucial. We may be impressed by their muscle, but we also fear it. It is also the case that, as we have seen their influence extend beyond the purely industrial and commercial context, we have come to expect more from them. They are a *social* force and we expect them to play a responsible social role. One of the spin-offs of this can be the sometimes misplaced faith in the ability – and right – of business to act like government. But we have already pointed out that business, as business, is not the same as government. Another, more legitimate, claim is that such a powerful social force ought to be responsible in the use of its power and that means being accountable to a public wider than merely a board of directors. Thus has corporate governance, even if not immediately recognisable to everyone by that name, become an issue of public interest and discussion.

WHAT *IS* CORPORATE GOVERNANCE?

Although changes in forms of 'corporate governance' are now almost routinely recommended as the answer to problems of corporate control, the concept itself is often misunderstood and misrepresented. It is, as Irving Shapiro says, 'not a subject with a single meaning, but . . . a shorthand label for an array of social and political as well as economic concerns'.[1] The difficulty here is that corporate governance can become confused with public policy or economic theory or political ideology. But corporate governance is not the same as the encouragement of business to

[1] I. Shapiro, Power and accountability: the changing role of the Corporate Board of Directors, quoted in W. Hoffman and J. Moore, *Business Ethics*, McGraw-Hill, 1990, p. 219.

promote the general public interest or support democratic structures; or the enjoining of shareholders to advance the government's industrial policy.

If, however, we start, as ever, from the business aim, we can
specify and limit the parameters of corporate governance, and
the ethical issues involved here, as almost entirely concerned
with ways of making sure that directors and management are
accountable to shareholders. Understood thus, corporate governance should not start from preoccupations with putting employees
on the board or insisting on the 'duty' of institutional shareholders
to be tough with directors; it is not the principal corporate
purpose to give people wider experience of self-government or
the taste for power – except in so far as these enhance longer-term
owner value. Rather it must begin by identifying the corporate
responsibilities of all stakeholders. Corporate governance, then,
seeks to establish the control systems which will allow such
responsibilities, on the parts of all stakeholders, to be fulfilled.

It is worth mentioning at this point, too, that corporate governance is viewed differently in different countries and even in
different sectors of the economy in the same country. The reception of the Cadbury Report in the UK, for example, has shown
how different are the approaches here of businesses in the industrial and financial sectors to the role of the board and the
relationships between the major stakeholders. In other countries
too, the nature of corporate governance is largely dictated by their
conventional industrial relationships. In Germany, this involves a
two-tier board structure where the supervisory board (*Aufsichtsrat*)
oversees the management board (*Vorstand*) and Works Councils
have wide rights to information and consultation on remuneration, conditions of employment, etc.[2] This system certainly, in
theory, allows a fair degree of accountability but it is argued by
some that the *Aufsichtsrat* is often either too weak to assert its
powers or so strong that it simply impedes essential decisions.[3]
The important point, however, is that the board structure here
cannot be taken out of the context of German industrial legislation, union practice and Works Council influence, all of which

[2] For a short account of the German and American board systems, see J. P. Charkham,
   Effective Boards, Institute of Chartered Accountants, 1986, pp. 59–62.
[3] Charkham, *Effective Boards*, p. 61.

affect the way in which corporate governance is viewed and the relationships between stakeholders considered. Again, the role of the banks in supporting German business, largely the result of Germany's post-war reconstruction effort, has been important and allows supervisory boards, on which banks are represented, to have a powerful influence on management board decisions.

In Japan, the supervisory role of boards is weak by European standards in that they do not oversee management, as they are largely composed of senior executive management. It is sometimes argued that the Japanese long-term commitment to business decisions and projects is partly the result of a system where the short-term demands of shareholders for their return on investment are less influential than in the West, and where senior management's preferred focus on longer-term growth can therefore become company strategy.

In the USA, there are fewer laws and regulations affecting business than elsewhere, although Federal legislation exists on such issues as competition policy and insider trading. Boards are unitary (not two-tier) and tend to have a majority of non-executive directors.[4] The audit committee, mandatory since 1977 for all quoted businesses, has to be made up of non-executives and board remuneration committees often are too. This emphasis on non-executives is one picked up by the Cadbury Committee, which suggests that 'outside' or 'independent' directors should have a stronger role to play in ensuring the accountability of management in British business.

A PROBLEM FOR CORPORATE GOVERNANCE?

If the main ethical dilemma for corporate governance is the question of accountability, of who has power to do what and how that power is constrained, there is a further problem in the very aim of business itself. The achievement of the business aim requires strong strategic direction, and sometimes practices which seem to advance that aim may be undermining of strict accountability. For example, it is often argued that, in the pursuit of long-term owner value, management needs to be able to protect itself from the threat of takeover, say by special shareholding

---

[4] Charkham, *Effective Boards*, pp. 57–9.

arrangements or restrictive voting procedures.[5] These may give management more strategic control but they can also work against the attempt to make it accountable to other stakeholders, especially shareholders. It was the recognition of this fact, among others, that led the Cadbury Committee to emphasise that it should 'be recognised that no system of control can eliminate the risk of fraud without so shackling companies as to impede their ability to compete in the market place'.[6] However, the trend towards greater accountability is strong all over Europe. Both national and EU regulations have challenged protection for managements if these are seen to limit the ability of shareholders to oversee their investment. Where there is a legal or regulatory requirement to disclose information or to act in an open, transparent way, this will, of course, be required of the ethical organisation. Business will typically obey the law, without which its very existence is in question. Where 'best practice' also emerges on the side of accountability and transparency, it will probably be in the interest of the achievement of the business aim to accept it. No reputable business these days can afford to look secretive with its shareholders or over-protective of its management, and long-term owner value is unlikely to be served by giving this impression. Where business ethics and corporate governance come together is in ensuring that all stakeholders in the business fulfil their proper corporate responsibilities. It is worth starting, then, by looking at the corporation and the business aim and then at the roles and responsibilities of the board (including non-executive directors) and of shareholders.

CORPORATE GOVERNANCE AND THE BUSINESS AIM

In this book, we have talked about 'business' as the general term for the activity in which we are interested and of which corporations are only one kind. 'Corporate governance' relates, by

[5] There are many forms of defensive strategy: for example, 'shark repellants' such as staggered boards which stops a bidder gaining complete control; 'supermajority' which involves the requirement for a high percentage (say, 80 per cent) of shares needed to approve a merger; 'poison pills', where shareholders have convertible stock which must be repurchased by the acquirer. For these and other defences, see R. Brealey and S. Myers, *Principles of Corporate Finance*, McGraw-Hill, 1988, pp. 813–4.

[6] Report of the Committee on the Financial aspects of Corporate Governance, Gee & Co. Ltd, December 1992, p. 12.

definition, to corporations and so we will take them as the focus of this chapter. Very many businesses, in any case, take the form of corporations, and the principles and best practices developed in the course of the corporate governance debate tend, in many cases, to become the recommended ones for all businesses.

Corporations are legal entities, created for a purpose (not necessarily that of doing business) which, in the UK, must be specified in the Memorandum of Association. Corporations normally have limited liability and shareholders are the collective owners of the corporation, who require a return for their risk (via dividends and/or capital gain) and control (via voting rights at the Annual General Meeting for instance). They technically own the corporation and it is to them, through the board, that management is responsible. It is thus their responsibility to keep the corporation on course towards its declared ends, for which the shareholder capital was originally given.

Implicit in the corporation's purpose too is the assumption of long-term existence, and this in turn requires that the organisation operate to maintain confidence, both within the corporation and outside it.

Again, the requirements of ordinary decency – honesty, fairness and the like – are, as we have argued, central to the achievement of the corporate aim. The shareholders in the corporation will therefore act accordingly and make sure that their agents, the board and management, carry these principles through in their corporate action. And since the aims of the corporation are most likely to be achieved not only by decency in its dealings but by justice in the awarding of remunerations or responsibilities or contracts, so rewards should follow contribution to the corporate aim. Ordinary decency and distributive justice are, then, the central ethical principles of corporate governance, just as we have seen they are of other aspects of business ethics.

Corporations may not, as we have said, have a business aim. They may, for example, be charities or 'not for profit'. But, to the extent that the corporation *is* a business, its aim will be the achievement of long-term owner value, subject to the constraints of justice and common decency. And this is important in determining the proper roles of shareholders and of boards. If a corporation claims to be a business, solicits funds from shareholders, hires employees, and commissions suppliers on that basis, it gives these stakeholders the reasonable expectation that it will act like a business and that its aim is indeed long-term owner value. If, however, it then proceeds to act as a charity or a social-interest group, then those stakeholders will have been deceived in these reasonable expectations. However worthy the charitable cause or compelling the social interest, the business aim will not be achieved and people will have been let down accordingly.

THE ROLE OF THE BOARD

Given that the business corporation has specified its aim, what is the role of the board? It is there to identify and ensure the development of strategy; to recruit the top management to carry through that strategy; and to ensure that it has the financial and other resources to pursue the strategy. In all these aims, the members of the board are obliged, as trustees, to protect shareholders' funds. In the UK, there is only one board and one class of director, all of whom, executive and non-executive, share board responsibilities.

As well as its strategic function, the board is also there to perform a representative function: it is there to reconcile potential conflicts between the corporation's stakeholders. It is sometimes suggested that, if this representative function is to be a reality, then principal stakeholders must have a seat on the board. This is not the case. To begin with, the idea of the board as a collegiate unit is strongly implied in the unitary boards of the UK (and of the US and Canada too) and the idea of representative directors who owe a specific allegiance to outside interests cuts across this unitary principle. The idea of employee directors, for example, has often been rejected for just this reason. Not that the interests of employees are considered irrelevant to the achievement of the business aim; far from it. But the notion of a worker-director whose job it is to represent the company's employees, and who is specifically delegated to do so, is hard to reconcile with that of a unitary board all of whose members should be moving to a collective view of the best interest of the business.[7] The notion of a unitary board allows for and indeed

---

[7] For a discussion on the worker-director concept, see Employees as directors, *Financial Times*, 4 December 1990.

requires different perspectives to be raised and different interests and views to be taken into account but it does not allow for a mandated representative delegated by a particular group to represent their interests regardless of the board view of the interests of the whole.

It has also to be said that taking on the representative role is not something that many important stakeholders are keen to do. The unions are often dubious about taking on this kind of very public responsibility when they can probably have more influence out of the glare of publicity. Again, institutional shareholders, who are often thought to have the clout to make an impact on board policy, are frequently uncertain about the wisdom of seeking seats on the boards of companies in their portfolios in case they expose themselves to charges of conflict of interest (insider dealing and so on).

But the representative function of the board can be fulfilled without the actual representatives of stakeholders being there in person. The law, for example, in some cases holds directors to be responsible for infringements of the rights of stakeholders and, in the interests of the business aim, they will not then ignore these various claims in making their decisions about the whole. Ultimately, however, the board is there to make decisions about the direction of the business as a whole; all views which are relevant to such decisions should be taken into account, but no one interest group should be allowed to dominate them.

A further function of the board is that of oversight of the management of the corporation. The board is legally responsible for the business's activities and has, in some circumstances, a fiduciary duty to shareholders and other stakeholders. There is potentially a conflict here for boards between taking the strategic view and knowing enough about the day-to-day operations of the company to be able to challenge management if need be. In the last resort, the board has to be able to get rid of the chief executive (or any other of the senior management team) if it judges that this is in the interests of the business and, as we shall see in looking at the role of non-executive directors, this is not without its difficulties. The crucial thing here is that the whole board has sufficient information to be able to oversee management, not to second-guess it, but to call it to account for its actions. The main functions of the board are positive rather than negative: to advise and warn and to give a broader perspective to decisions on the basis of collective wide experience. As Jonathan Charkham says, 'The acid test of a board is whether it has the authority *if necessary* to hold the chief executive in check: the value of a good board goes far beyond this. It provides the man at the top with a bank of *committed* talent.'[8]

NON-EXECUTIVE DIRECTORS

The term 'non-executive director' is probably something of a misnomer. By emphasising what they are not, it suggests that such board members are less significant than executives and are therefore second-class board citizens. For this reason, Sir Adrian Cadbury, whose committee on the Financial Aspects of Corporate Governance puts great emphasis on their role, suggests that they should be known as 'outside' or 'independent' directors. 'Independent directors would be the most expressive title and would automatically separate those who were independent from those who had some link with the company, other than their board membership.'[9] On the other hand, if non-executives do not in fact have teeth, no mere change of name is going to give them these. Ross Perot referred to them, somewhat disparagingly, as management's 'pet rocks': yet these very non-executives, of whom Mr Perot was one at General Motors until 1986, were instrumental in limiting management's power there in 1992.[10] And in the UK, it was non-executives, with shareholder support, who removed the Chairman of the Burton Group and of Barclays Bank and encouraged the Chairman of BP to stand down.

What is the role of non-executives in the ethical enterprise and are they capable of performing that role? Their role is to bring together, as far as possible, the interests of those who run the company and those who own it. It may seem that there should be little between these two positions, for both are committed to the creation of a successful business: the board, and particularly the management team, so that their jobs and their own remuneration should be secure and the shareholders so that they can

[8] Charkham, *Effective Boards*, p. 10.
[9] Sir Adrian Cadbury writing in Pro-NED's 9th Annual Review, September 1991, p. 3.
[10] In search of better boardrooms, *The Economist*, 30 May 1992, p. 13.

maximise the returns on their investments. However, there are sometimes differences of perspective here in what has been called short-termism – or 'now-nowism' as it is sometimes known.[11] Owners, it is claimed, look for shorter term returns, which may undermine management's longer term planning and investment – or the other way round. For it can also be argued, and has been recently, that it is not the shareholders but the managers whose outlook is too short term; it is they who want to talk about break-evens and short pay-back periods in order to secure their own compensation and bonuses. Institutional shareholders at least, on the other hand, are much more likely to look for long-term income streams.[12] Either way, one may say, the interests of owner and manager may conflict and it is one job of the non-executive to keep in mind all the time the business aim, the creation of long-term owner value, in terms of which to bring excessively short-term management or shareholder thinking into line.

Can non-executives do this successfully? This will depend on a number of things, including the quality of these directors themselves, how they are recruited, their access to information, and their standing with the board and, particularly, the chairman of the board. Cadbury recommends a strengthening of the non-executive role, insists that they be truly independent and that significant decisions be taken by the whole board and not simply presented by the executives as *faits accomplis*, but this would require a considerable tightening up on most current practice. For example, Cadbury's Code of Best Practice, published along with the Report on the Financial Aspects of Corporate Governance, states that non-executives should be 'of sufficient calibre and number for their views to carry significant weight in the board's decisions'.[13] It goes on to specify that they should be consulted on 'issues of strategy, performance, resources, including key appointments, and standards of conduct'. They should also be 'independent of management and free from any business or

---

[11] This was the term coined by Richard Darman, a member of President Bush's cabinet. See report in *The Independent*, 21 August 1989, p. 19.
[12] See, for example, P. Marsh, *Short-Termism on Trial*, Institutional Fund Managers' Association, 1990. Also A. Clements, Why perception and reality do not tally, *Financial Times*, 22 July 1991, p. 9.
[13] Cadbury, *The Code of Best Practice*, (Para. 1.3) p. 6.

other relationships which could materially interfere with the exercise of their independent judgement', 'be appointed for specified terms ... (and) selected through a formal process ... [which] should be a matter for the board as a whole'.[14] If all this could be achieved, the chance of non-executives upholding the business aim, which is their main ethical role, would be much enhanced.

However, recent UK research findings on non-executives seem to show that, as currently recruited and used, they cannot play the role identified by Cadbury. Even in larger companies, executives heavily outweigh non-executives.[15] Chairmen are the only group with a majority (62 per cent) who believe that the contribution of non-executives is very effective (perhaps because they largely appoint the non-executives on their boards); only a third of chief executives hold the same view and indeed a minority of non-executives themselves (45 per cent) concur.[16] Executive directors, in general, have a poor opinion of their non-executive colleagues, suggesting, *inter alia,* that they 'fail to understand the business', 'are of lightweight calibre' and even 'they consider it a pension policy not a job'.[17] Non-executives, on the other hand, seem to believe that they often do not get co-operation or respect from the executives: 'NEDs (non-executives) can suffer disillusionment if their endeavours to assist ... are rebuffed or, more likely, ignored. It is executive directors who fail NEDs more often than vice versa.'[18]

Selection and appointment processes would seem to do little to give confidence to those who run the company when only 23 per cent of companies drew up a candidate/job profile for non-executive appointments. In addition, in half the companies researched, the chairman already had an individual in mind who was approached. In 37 per cent of cases, chairmen said they informally consulted contacts and more than half also said that, in the end, it was the chairman who made the appointment, with final board approval.[19] On appointment, fewer than a third of non-executives were given any written clarification of their

---

[14] Cadbury, *Code*, paras. 2.1–2.4, pp. 6–7.
[15] Research into the Role of the Non-Executive Director, Pro-NED, July 1992, Executive summary, p. 6.
[16] Ibid., p. 8.
[17] Ibid., p. 9.
[18] Ibid., p. 9.
[19] Ibid., p. 10.

role or responsibilities and it is perhaps not surprising, therefore, that there is wide scope for misunderstanding among board members.

If non-executives are to do any thing like the job Cadbury, with the right instincts, prescribes for them, these factors and others will have to be taken into account. There should be, at a minimum, a proper job description, search and shortlisting; a letter of appointment identifying the requirements of the job; an induction programme introducing the new director into the business; and a code of practice to identify best practice and underline the serious and professional nature of the role.

Cadbury is also surely right to emphasise the importance of the audit committee, which he believes should be composed solely of non-executives, in scrutinising the figures and recommending the appointment of the auditors. This not only raises the board's perception of non-executives but gives them access to information which in turn allows them to ask the questions they need answered if they are to pursue their part in ensuring the business aim of securing longer term owner value.

There remains the question of whether there are sufficient numbers of candidates of the required calibre to do the job. There is no doubt that many non-executives believe that they are fobbed off with cosmetic answers to their questions and that executives in the business do not rate them very highly. The attitude, as one describes it, can be 'Management knows best – we don't need to explain.'[20] But if non-executives were sufficiently heavyweight, would they be willing to accept this response and, indeed, would executives dare to be so cavalier in their responses? It is certainly the case that research has shown that 76 per cent of companies (and 92 per cent of institutional investors and auditors) believe that it is fairly or very difficult to find non-executives of calibre.[21]

But this view may be at least partially the result of a misunderstanding of what the non-executive job is about. It is not about trying, and failing, to fill the executive role. Its value is in its independence. Non-executives are not involved in the day-to-day running of the business. This therefore allows them a certain

[20] J. Shively, Confessions of a non-executive, *Financial Times*, 15 July 1991, p. 11.
[21] Pro-NED, p. 12.

perspective, a more objective overall view of the company. They do not need to be as professionally qualified in finance as the finance director or in R&D as the development director. Indeed, if they were, they might well slip into the second-guessing business. But they may and should, in addition to asking questions about strategy and finance, raise, say, the consumer perspective or environmental issues which may impinge very directly on long-term owner value, but which do not immediately suggest themselves to those with a more specific, functional expertise. If boards thought more about the job description of non-executives in such terms, more people might be considered to have the experience, judgement and plain common sense which make a good non-executive. In any case, only if the board as a whole is clear about the business aim and the independent directors' essential contribution to it, can non-executives do their job.

SHAREHOLDER POWER

Shareholders are the owners of the business. It is to them that management and board owe their commitment to protect the long-term value of their investment. It is often suggested, therefore, that, from the point of view of corporate governance, the role of the shareholder should be in the active overseeing of the management and board. As an extension of this, it is suggested that shareholders have a *duty* to long-term investment in companies; that there is an ethical issue here about corporate loyalty, as if buying shares in order to sell when it seems opportune is not acceptable. Again, however, clarifying the nature and ends of the corporation and the role of the shareholder makes the position clearer.

Business corporations exist to produce long-term owner value. People buy shares to secure financial gain; to this extent, buying and selling is not an ethical decision at all but a matter of weight of advantage: whether the value of retaining the shares is thought likely to be greater than the value of selling. There is no moral obligation to go on being a shareholder regardless of the value of the shares. Corporate loyalty cannot require that shareholders stay with the company even when it is not producing value; what it can and should require is that shareholders make sure that the company keeps to its end of securing shareholder value. It is then most likely that shareholders will see the advantage of remaining as shareholders. As one commentator says, 'If a shareholder acts responsibly as a shareholder, and holds the corporation to its proper ends, then the corporation will be more likely to merit and attract his continued investment.'[22] It is, in effect, a virtuous circle.

But most individual shareholders feel very insignificant in the face of huge, or even medium-size companies. How can they monitor the management's performance or have an influence on the direction the board sets? In principle, they have voting rights at General Meetings. They can refuse to underwrite the decisions of the board or even appointments to the board. And they do sometimes manage to band together and use their power. Recently, for example, small shareholders in a Belgian tourism company got a court order compelling the French company which had made a bid to take them over to supply more information about the negotiations.[23] In some cases, then, small shareholders who act in concert can have an impact. Extending this experience, is there a case, as is sometimes suggested, for wider share ownership?

There may be – from the point of view of politicians who make political capital from this populist cry, or stockbrokers who may believe that individual punters are a soft touch for the hard sell. But from the point of view of the business aim, wider share ownership is hardly relevant. Just as long-term investors do not guarantee a healthier business, neither does a large number of investors. The significant issue in whether shareholders play a useful role in achieving the business end is not numbers but knowledge of the company. What is necessary, it has recently been suggested, is 'involved shareholders . . . who have a direct interest in the company's fate'. [24]

If involved and informed shareholders are what is required, are institutional shareholders the answer? More and more of

---

[22] E. Sternberg, The responsible shareholder, *Business Ethics*, vol. 1, no. 3, July 1992, p. 197.

[23] The case of Wagon-Lits against Accor, a French hotel group. Report in the *Economist*, 30 November 1991, p. 82.

[24] Never mind the width, *The Economist*, 30 March 1991, p. 16.

them are being encouraged to take a lead in improving the corporate governance of companies in both the US and the UK.[25] And institutions are more and more powerful in their share of the equity market. In the 1950s, for example, individuals held over 70 per cent of shares on the British stock market while institutions held less than 20 per cent. By 1990, the positions were more or less reversed. The Association of British Insurers, for example, has recommended that institutional investors, with this amount of power, take a more active role in the companies in which they invest.[26] But institutional investors are not, it is sometimes claimed, the owners of the company but only the *agents* of the owners. The real owners are the beneficiaries of the pension fund or unit trust. Do the institutions, then, have a right to oversee companies and, even more importantly, are they best placed to do so? Many institutional shareholders might, for example, fear conflicts of interest in getting too close to companies (on the board, for example) in which they invest, risking charges of acquiring market-sensitive information. On the other hand, not to be close enough may mean being a pretty weak protector of owner value. In rare cases where institutional shareholders have stood up for their investors' interest, the results have not been uniformly successful.

The case of Tace, a British firm making environmental control equipment, is an example of some of the practical difficulties faced by institutional investors, even when they are prepared to commit themselves to defending their investment directly by opposing management decisions. The Norwich Union chief investment officer, Michael Sandland (who was also Chairman of the Institutional Shareholders Committee), was widely praised for his stand against what was seen as the inefficiency and arrogance of the Tace management. In the end, however, only one other institution agreed to help pay the bill in legal and other costs which resulted from the fight to replace the top management.[27] Sandland's view is that institutional shareholders are not as powerful as they might appear, partly because of the secrecy in which such battles are conducted and partly as a result of the

[25] Investors wake up to their power, *Financial Times*, 3 December 1990, p. 13.
[26] *Financial Times*, 15 March 1991, p. 8.
[27] See report in *Financial Times*, 6 April 1992, p. 12.

lack of resources available to fund managers to engage in them. Institutions are unlikely, therefore, to use their power by engaging in concerted action. 'You are unlikely to get some kind of pan-institutional framework because shareholders are unwilling to surrender to a third party their proxy rights.'[28]

WHISTLE-BLOWING

However difficult it may be to set up the arrangements whereby board directors and shareholders ensure that the business aim is being appropriately pursued, it is the task of corporate govern-ance to explore better structures and systems to this end. It is not only shareholders and boards who have a role here but also employees, who may often be in a position to see, more directly than the other two groups, what is actually going on in the company. What if employees see things which they believe to be wrong in the way the company operates? What should they do? Whom should they tell? Should they tell at all? These are some of the dilemmas of whistle-blowing where an individual is faced with a conflict of loyalties and often no clear structures within which to organise a response.

In British society, there is an inbuilt aversion to anything which smacks of 'sneaking'. From schooldays on, those who 'tell on' others tend to be ostracised and 'informer' is always a pejorative term. Yet there may be cases when an employee believes it would be wrong to keep silent and the taboo against informing should be broken. The difficulty is in determining in which cases this is really justified (or even obligatory) and how it should be done.

Typically, employees are taken to owe a duty of loyalty and confidentiality to the business which employs them. Whistle-blowing outside the business (*external* whistle-blowing) is liable to damage the business and to increase the likelihood of retali-ation against the whistle-blower which, in turn, increases his risk and makes him perhaps less likely to go public. *Internal* whistle-blowing, by going to a senior colleague within the busi-ness, may equally meet with suspicion and uncertainty.

But do employees really have a duty of loyalty to the business

[28] *Financial Times*, 6 April 1992.

regardless of how the business is operating? Clearly not.[29] The
law, for example, is clear that, if something illegal is going on,
there is no duty of confidentiality and no business can, by implicit
or explicit means, tie its employees to silence regardless of the
situation. Where an employee *does* have a loyalty to the business
is in making sure that the business aim is fulfilled. Ordinarily,
this will mean not giving support to its competitors by embarrass-
ing the business in any way; but this does not preclude whistle-
blowing. For the aims of the business will probably not be served
by wrongdoing. Being loyal to the business is not saying nothing,
regardless of what one sees. Being loyal is protecting the things
which allow the business to achieve shareholder value over the
long term: its reputation, and concern for its products, customers
and employees.

So when is whistle-blowing justifiable? When the business aim
is being undermined by activity in the business rather than
served by it. And is it ever *obligatory* to blow the whistle? This
may be ethically more complex. For whistle-blowing to be a duty
rather than simply justifiable would require that there was a
general moral obligation to others here. If it is established that
there is clear danger of harm to others in the continuity of the
activity, then there would seem to be a positive moral obligation
to blow the whistle. The criterion of harm would not only
necessarily apply to immediate physical harm but to longer term
harm to welfare or quality of life. In other words, it was obligatory
to blow the whistle in the case of the potentially lethal design
fault on the Ford Pinto; but it would have been obligatory too
if one had known about the fraudulent practices of a Robert
Maxwell which would eat up people's pensions and take away
their security and peace of mind.

Whistle-blowing is therefore justifiable and may even be obligatory. This, of course, presupposes that as soon as the problem
is pointed out within the business it is not immediately dealt
with and put right. Before the whistle is blown externally, the
internal routes should be carefully considered. This may involve
reporting to a superior or to an officer of the company specially

[29] This is not the view of, for example, Richard de George, who argues that strict criteria
need to be applied for whistle-blowing to be morally justified, exactly because it *is* a
form of disloyalty. See R. T. de George, *Business Ethics*, Macmillan, 1986, p. 213.

deputed to look at such concerns. Whatever methods are available for allowing the issue to be dealt with inside the business should be tried so that breach of confidentiality and potential harm to the business from going public may be averted.

Sadly, it is true that whistle-blowers are not generally well treated. Often their claims are disregarded or trivialised; their motives are called in question; and they may be stigmatised as troublemakers (like the 'sneaks' at school) and passed over for promotion or even fired. The arrangements which the business makes to deal with employee concerns of this kind are, therefore, crucial. Proper corporate arrangements will indicate to employees that the company takes this kind of ethical concern very seriously, as well as encouraging people to come forward rather than immediately raising the stakes by going public. An internal ombudsman or operational auditor, accessible to all staff and reporting to the board, provides the kind of arrangement which could help mistakes to be rectified and malpractice to be dealt with, with the minimum of harm to all stakeholders. Richard de George suggests that this kind of arrangement, with an 'inspector general', independent of management and reporting to the audit committee of the board, should be required by law for all companies of a certain size.[30] And such mechanisms are not only abstract ideas. The John Lewis Partnership, for example, has thirty-two registrars, independent of management, who deal with employees' concerns about unethical or dishonest behaviour and report directly to the company's chairman.[31]

Just as it is important, from the point of view of business ethics, to be clear about what makes whistle-blowing justifiable or even required, so it is important to understand what does not, but may be thought to, affect its justification. While it is true that the whistle-blower who clearly acts purely from disinterested motives will probably command more credibility and respect than one who has an axe to grind, still the whistle-blowing is justified if it identifies wrongdoing regardless of the motives of the whistle-blower. As pointed out in part I, attitudes and actions can be distinguished and it is the actions which are relevant from the point of view of business ethics. In deciding whether

---

[30] De George, *Business Ethics* p. 216.
[31] Dare you blow the whistle? *The Times*, 22 October 1992, p. 10.

someone is a good *person* rather than whether their action was justifiable, one would, of course, have to take their motivation into account; but the action remains a good action if it identifies wrong or prevents harm. Even if it looks as if someone is acting from spite, where, say, they have been passed over for promotion or fired by the company, there is all the more reason to beware dismissing their claim simply because of their imputed motivation. They may have uncovered a genuine problem for the company and the probable reasons for their revealing it now should not be allowed to obscure this possibility and its prompt investigation. Motivation, in this case, where the good of the business is involved, may be an *ex post facto* explanation of why an unsubstantiated allegation was made but should not be taken as proof in advance that a claim is unjustifiable.

In the end, the corporate response to whistle-blowing should be to welcome and encourage the impulse to identify wrongdoing in the business – and also to set up mechanisms which will make it, as far as possible, unnecessary for employees to go public with their concern about dishonest or unethical behaviour. If something is genuinely amiss, it is only to the business's advantage to know about it and put it right before it becomes (more) counter-productive to the business aim. If such situations can be identified through channels within the business itself, so that unfavourable publicity and costly crisis management can be avoided, so much the better.

THE ENDS OF CORPORATE GOVERNANCE

Although the current concern of business with corporate governance is partly the outcome of its concern with its own rather tarnished image over the past few years and in particular the stigma that has attached to business as a whole after episodes such as the Maxwell affair, still the roots of the issue go deeper than this. They go deeper, too, than concerns about executive pay or insider trading. There has been a niggling worry since at least the beginning of the twentieth century, when owners of businesses largely ceased to be also their managers, about the gap between shareholders and management and the effect this may have on business performance. This was finally and starkly illustrated for many people in the hostile takeovers of the 1980s, where shareholders who wanted immediate returns opposed managements who claimed long-term strategies in a bid to keep their jobs.

At another level, the enormous increase in institutional shareholding, and the way in which fund managers feel compelled to invest proportionately in companies that make up share indices, means that such owners will be inclined to stay and fight directly, often with the board, rather than sell. The board, particularly its non-executive directors, is supposed to look after shareholders' interests and auditors are supposed to let shareholders know whether the company's accounts are correct, at least in outline. That is the theory but there is concern that none of it is working well. Non-executives are largely nominated and appointed by the executives whose performance they are meant to monitor; boards are made up of a majority of the senior management who are meant to be overseen for the shareholder by those very boards; institutional investors are unwilling to take an active role in protecting shareholder interests and may not, in any case, know much about business; auditors are often too close to the management and so on and so on.

The Cadbury Committee makes some useful suggestions about giving non-executives real power and making the audit committee genuinely independent. It also suggests that listed companies should be required to indicate whether they are meeting these conditions in the hope that the unwilling will be shamed into doing so. But the critical issue of how to mobilise shareholder support for the boards which are supposed to look after owner interests remains largely untackled. Strategies which have been suggested include contributions by institutions to the funding of professional directors who would intervene directly in the management of companies or the pooling of institutional shares so that a non-executive could be nominated on the strength of the combined holding. In the end, however, none of these is likely to be the final answer to the corporate governance conundrum, which will be best dealt with, if never permanently solved, by bearing in mind always the business aim and the need for all members of the corporation to be focused on the achievement of owner value.

PART III

The ethical organisation

9

The ethical audit

Pay particular attention to follow-up: there is no point in
knowing what is wrong if nothing happens to fix it.

(Frances Cairncross, *Costing the Earth*)

The internal control system is the whole system . . . established by management to carry on the business of the
enterprise in an orderly and efficient manner [and] ensure
adherence to management policies.

(Auditing Guideline 308, Guidelines for Internal
Auditors, Auditing Practices Committee (1990))[1]

'If you can't count it, you can't manage it.' So goes the thinking
behind much financial auditing practice. And although this view
can be parodied as the notion that *all* there is to managing is
knowing the numbers, it is true that if the systems which allow
us to monitor financial movement in the business are not in
place we don't have control of the business. The internal financial
audit is seen as being required in order to ensure that the
company's financial and accounting systems 'are providing accurate and up-to-date information on its current financial position'
and that 'the company's published financial statements represent
a true and fair reflection of this position.'[2] The external audit
reviews this process and comments on its satisfactoriness.

In recent years, the importance of the auditing process has been
recognised and emphasised, partly as one practical response to the
various financial scandals with which business has been faced and
partly as the interactive nature of such processes has been acknow-
leged: the failures of the past can and should be the warnings of the
present which inform the good practice of the future.

[1] Quoted in *A Framework for Internal Control*, Chartered Institute of Management Accountants, 1992, p. 1.
[2] Audit Committees, Pro-Ned, March 1993, p. 3.

153

So far there has been little in the way of a specifically *ethical* auditing process. It might be argued that this is because the whole area is inappropriate for this kind of approach. Ethics is, after all, qualitative and not quantitative: values can be judged but they cannot be weighed or empirically tested. However, as audits have moved on from the purely financial context to, for example, the environmental or the organisational, this assumption may be seen as less well founded. As I shall argue, there may be much to be gained from an audit of an organisation's ethics and values. The process may not be straightforward but this is, in itself, no reason to reject it as impossible.

OTHER TYPES OF AUDIT

If an audit is a way of finding out whether, in practice, the business's systems and structures are achieving its goals, then the purpose of auditing is to establish how far the financial or organisational or environmental strategy is being successfully put into practice throughout the business. The extension of audit beyond financial audit is already well established in North America and in some larger European concerns, where the audit committee of the board may have had its brief extended initially to cover issues like compliance with laws and regulations, and insurance, both of which, if not properly monitored, may involve the business in serious financial exposure. The committee is asked to review, from time to time, the business's procedures and comment on their adequacy. In some cases, environmental risk has been added to the committee's remit since failure to comply with environmental laws, greatly expanded in recent legislation, could be extremely expensive for a business.

Environmental auditing

If we take environmental auditing, for example, this attempts to use a systematic approach to all aspects of the business's manufacturing, office and field safety procedures to analyse their effect on the environment and to generate ideas about how harmful effects can be minimised. As one practitioner suggests, 'Although, like financial audit, it provides a snapshot of the organisation at one time, the environmental audit is different in that it is intended to force positive change. Attention is directed not simply at the environmental bottom line, but to every point where the organisation may have a negative impact on the environment.'[3]

Concentrating specifically on the company's impact on the environment may reveal areas where policy modifications or systematic structural changes may be necessary. Environmental policy in the organisation, in whatever form it has hitherto existed, can then be refined to focus on those issues which are revealed as particularly relevant, or particularly weak, for this business. The audit may also reveal the extent to which existing policy is being operationalised, both identifying shortcomings and pinpointing good practice for the future. Businesses differ in the focus of their environmental impact: manufacturing will be different in this respect from service industry. Yet, although the impact of manufacturing on such hazards as air and water pollution or disposal of toxic substances may be obvious, the environmental significance of other areas should not be overlooked. The assumption that it is only heavy industry which pollutes is quite wrong and audits in sectors such as distribution or retailing will need to identify their own particular auditing checklist. Not only solid waste disposal and spill prevention, but, for example, packaging and product safety may emerge as central to the exercise. The oil firm Texaco has regular audits of its UK operations. These include not only monitoring water, air and solid waste pollution, but the use of hazardous substances such as asbestos and CFCs. Compliance with safety regulations, both internal and external, is also reviewed. Any deficiencies are noted and action is taken to remedy them.[4] In her environmental checklist for companies, Frances Cairncross suggests that, having drafted a policy and publicised it, a business should institute 'a regular audit to check on what is happening'. She goes on, 'Pay particular attention to follow-up: there is no point in knowing what is wrong if nothing happens to fix it.'[5]

Organisational auditing

Organisational audits have been put in place in a number of businesses with the aim of identifying improvements which can

[3] D. Clutterbuck and D. Snow, *Working with the Community*, Weidenfeld and Nicolson, 1990, p. 148.
[4] Clutterbuck and Snow, *Working with the Community*, p. 150.
[5] F. Cairncross, *Costing the Earth*, Business Books, 1991, p. 252.

be made in the way the business operates and in the service it delivers. The King's Fund, for example, a healthcare charity, has operated an organisational audit for health service providers since 1989. The setting and monitoring of standards in this case is done on a national basis and a number of District Health Authorities volunteered to pilot the programme if the King's Fund developed the standards. These standards have been modified and developed with the experience of doing the audit, so that the whole process is iterative. This is an important point to bear in mind for the ethical audit: the audit process is itself educational, and the findings at any stage, even if they point up shortcomings in an organisation, will be positive if they are fed back into the system in the form of changes in practice which improve performance.

In the case of the King's Fund audit, organisational standards have been derived which are applied to hospitals, providing a framework 'around which a hospital can demonstrate that it has an environment capable of supporting a high quality of clinical care. The standards developed . . . cover all services provided by the hospital.'[6] The standards relate to everything from the mission statement and the institution's objectives as set out in its business plan, to its service provision, management arrangements, communications, human resource policy, financial arrangements, policies and procedures. The evaluation of compliance with the standards (which are those the organisation itself aspires to in its mission and business plan) is measured largely by means of a survey conducted by healthcare professionals. It is emphasised at every point that the audit is part of an ongoing process, not an end in itself but rather 'a snapshot of how far we are towards achieving the standards'.[7]

IS AN *ETHICAL* AUDIT RELEVANT?

Even if audits of a business's financial, environmental and organisational arrangements may be useful, it does not, of course, necessarily follow that such a process is either suitable or relevant to ethics.

---

[6] Organisational Audit, Questions and Answers, The King's Fund, 1990.
[7] Organisational Audit.

Are values amenable at all to this kind of scrutiny? After all, it could be said, one cannot really identify the extent of a business's just dealings or common decency by counting instances or actions. On the other hand, if there is no way of seeing how and to what extent values are making a difference in the life of the business, is there any point in identifying them in the first place? If, as I have argued, business ethics makes a difference to the business's success, to the achievement of its aim, then we must surely at least try to identify what that difference is. And if values are not being carried through into action, that surely has to be specified and dealt with too. The trick will be to devise a framework which allows such factors to be identified and acted on, without assuming in any way that only numbers are what really count! In other words, the methodology here will be important (and probably eclectic).

Why is an ethical audit important? What will it contribute to the ethical progress of the business? Basically, it will contribute *three* things:

   it will make the business articulate its ethical priorities;
   it will make the business aware of its successes and short-
      comings;
   it will allow feedback and continuous improvement.

All of these are important. Many businesses now have a general statement of objectives, which in some cases is spelled out into a more comprehensive code of ethics or business principles. A detailed code may look, for example, at how the company's objectives will affect business relations with the company's major stakeholders. For example, in setting out a model code of ethics and good business practice, Clutterbuck and Snow suggest the following headings:

   objects of the business;
   customer relations (customer satisfaction and good faith in all
      agreements as well as fair pricing and after-sales service);
   shareholders (protection of investment and proper return);
   suppliers (co-operation long term, prompt settling of bills);
   employees (valuing of employees in recruitment, training,
      rewards, communication, conditions, safety, severance,
      etc.);
   the wider community (environmental, standards of safety, etc.,
      corporate policy on charitable giving, etc.);
   other issues (e.g. relations with competitors, research and devel-

opment policy, employee responsibilities – including conflicts of interests, confidentiality, equal opportunities, etc.).[8]
Such an outline is clearly abstract and the details of the code will depend on the business sector, its aim, its size and its culture. The Royal Dutch/Shell Group of Companies, for example, has a detailed principles statement which begins with a declaration of the business's objectives as 'to engage efficiently, responsibly and profitably in the oil, gas, chemicals, coal, metals and selected other businesses and to play an active role in the search for and development of other sources of energy. Shell companies seek a high standard of performance and aim to maintain a longterm position in their respective competitive environments.'[9] It goes on to state its responsibilities to shareholders, employees, customers and to society, underlining that its 'profitability is essential to discharging these responsibilities . . . it is a measure both of efficiency and of the ultimate value that people place on Shell products and services'. It also outlines, among other things, the company's code as a multinational company, its statement of business integrity, policy on the environment and open communications policy.

Articulating principles in this way will always be important for the business and its stakeholders and particularly so as the starting point of the audit process. The ethical audit which takes place against the background of an existing code will point up where the business is living out its code and where it is falling short. It is then essential, as Cairncross pointed out in the environmental context, to pay attention to follow-up – to putting things right or, at least, to putting in place an improvement programme. Audits are about getting to know what has worked and what has not and using feedback to move nearer to the goals of ethical behaviour in all the activities of the business.

THE BACKGROUND TO THE ETHICAL AUDIT

So, before the audit can proceed, the values of the business have to be made clear. These will emerge, to a large extent, from the aim of the particular business, its priorities and values as these

[8] Clutterbuck and Snow, *Working with the Community*, pp. 178–81.
[9] See S. Webley, *Company Philosophies and Codes of Business Ethics: A Guide to their Drafting and Use*, Institute of Business Ethics, 1988.

are spelled out in its principles and codes. If these do not yet exist in any expanded form, the mission statement or business plan may be a possible starting point in the identification of values.

Values need to be communicated if they are to have any significant impact on the operation of the business. Clearly established channels of communication are essential: there is no point in having a sophisticated ethical stance if only the director of human resources and the chairman know about it. Value statements and codes of ethics need to be endorsed and publicly supported by the board but they must also, to be effective, be owned and endorsed by everyone. They must be top-led but not top-down in any *dirigiste* sense. The need for good and clear communications of values is paramount, as is the need for constant feedback on how far the business has succeeded in putting these values into practice.

The practice is, of course, what it is all about. The creation of an impeccable code of ethics is of no avail if it simply sits on file, only to be brought out on ceremonial occasions, to display the ethical correctness of the board. The values of the business will not change – its commitment to honesty, integrity, justice, decency and the rest; but whether and how these are lived out in the activity of the business may be more problematic and the audit, properly used, may help in making the values a practical reality throughout the business.

The final background requirement to an ethical audit is the identification of the major stakeholders in the business and the ethical quality of relationships with them. All of this, the identification of values, the setting up of channels of communication, the focus on stakeholders, could, of course, be simply a sham, a bit of window-dressing in which the business indulges as a cheap piece of public relations. And, indeed, this is sometimes the criticism levelled at codes of ethics, value statements and the like, that they are meaningless exercises which disingenuously aim to convince people that something constructive has been done when there is, in fact, no substance there at all. There is always the danger too, that, even if it is not intended to deceive, the assumption may be that, once published, a code becomes an operational reality – the 'no sooner said than done' fallacy. Yet, as anyone with the slightest management experience knows only too well, the devil is in the implementation of policy rather than simply in its formulation and one would have to be very naive to believe otherwise. Again, if the motive for publishing a code of ethics is merely to be able to claim to be against sin, this is a dangerous ploy; for as soon as it becomes clear that you consistently fail to live up to your much-vaunted standards, the public relations effects are counter-productive. Both within and without the business, credibility will be badly wounded.

WHAT SHOULD AN ETHICAL AUDIT LOOK LIKE?

An ethical audit must, to be relevant, begin with the value statements and policies of the business. It should then aim to point up the extent to which structures and systems within the business support (or otherwise) these values. The difficulty is to identify the connection between the theory and the practice but this is the difficulty for management in any situation where strategy has to be put into practice. If ethical commitment is recognised as an important aspect of the achievement of the business aim, it becomes as crucial to implement the ethical strategy as to ensure the financial strategy. This may be difficult to implement and monitor in either case but it has to be attempted.

It has been a recurring theme of the argument of this book that, if ethical outcomes are sought, it is essential, as far as possible, to make the *right* thing the *easy* thing to do. To allow it to be easier to be dishonest – or at least to cut corners – than honest is a recipe for ethical uncertainty. Systems must be so arranged as to encourage doing the right thing and an audit may point to the areas where the implementation of values is being inhibited by the way in which systems operate.

Starting with the ethically significant policy statements will normally mean starting with the business's mission statement, statement of values or code of ethics, depending on what is in existence. As has been said, it has sometimes been suggested that codes of ethics are of dubious value when it comes to affecting business behaviour. And, of course, if there is no genuine commitment to stated values within a business, they will be likely to have little or no impact on behaviour. The viewing of codes as cosmetic, or as mere claims to be against sin, is a good way of ensuring that they will be treated as precisely that. Research in the USA in the early 1980s, for example, was very sceptical about whether codes were more than simply window-dressing.[10] As Laura Nash has said, 'Ethics codes were about as morally significant as a family of atheists putting up a Christmas tree for the kids in the month of December.'[11] However, over the last ten years, interest in ethical codes and belief in their central importance for the achievement of the business aim has been developing, not only in the USA but in Europe too. The Cadbury Committee on the Financial Aspects of Corporate Governance, for example, 'regard it as good practice for boards of directors to draw up codes of ethics or statements of business practice and to publish them both internally and externally'.[12] And as larger companies see the need to draw up such statements, the pressure will become greater on smaller ones to do so too. The Fortune 500 or the FTSE 100 may seem, in some ways, elite groups, but they are also, in many ways, exemplary cultures. What they do today, others do tomorrow. Awareness of the importance of publicly declared ethical commitments is an awareness of the *Zeitgeist*, not simply a passing fad, or a genuflection in the direction of today's fashion. But if these codes are to have practical meaning and are not just to be seen as optional extras, they must be shown to be part of the fabric of the business and integrated into its practice, not just an adjunct without operational significance. The only way in which this can be achieved is by constantly auditing the relationship between theory and practice.

To audit ethical practice in this way is not to suggest that there is an end to the process. Having identified the extent to which the practices of the business reflect and reinforce its stated values, the dialogue is only just beginning. An audit is not intended simply to point out strengths and weaknesses at this point, and leave it at that. It is, rather, the beginning of an iterative process where the publication and dissemination of audit

---

[10] See D. Cressey and C. Moore, *Corporate Codes of Ethical Conduct*, Peat Marwick and Mitchell Foundation, 1980.

[11] L. Nash, American and European corporate ethics practice: a 1991 survey, in J. Mahoney and E. Vallance, *Business Ethics in a New Europe*, Kluwer Academic Press, 1992, pp. 163–4.

[12] The Cadbury Report on the Financial Aspects of Corporate Government, para. 4.29.

findings should provoke awareness, discussion, suggestions for improvement and perhaps the setting of new targets of achievement within the organisation. These, in due course, will themselves be audited and further, clearer standards set, the aim always being to bring the value statements and the standards of practice more closely together.

This process is dialectical, not merely circular, since the idea is always to use the audit findings to improve business practice, which may then be pursued at a new level of awareness and in terms of more rigorous and specified targets and standards.

What would such an ethical audit look like? What questions would it ask? Clearly they will differ in detail from business to business, but there are some general issues which will be common to most, if not all, businesses of any size and complexity. An audit would surely, for example, have to enquire into the quality of the value statement itself. Is it clearly worded? Have contributions to the statement been sought from people at all levels in the business? Is it accessible and publicised both inside and outside the business? Is there clear and overt leadership from the very top in applying the values throughout the business?

The audit would surely also need to address service or product standards. Are they of the required quality for all stakeholders? Are the mechanisms in place to ensure the monitoring of this quality? Are the mechanisms in place to deal with problems in quality? Do people at all levels in the business know what these are?

Again, the audit would need to enquire into the appropriateness of management structures. Are lines of accountability and responsibility clear? Are the constitutional arrangements of the business documented and accessible? Do people know what is expected of them and are they enabled to do it? Is communication generally good within the business? Is communication with external stakeholders well developed?

The treatment of employees is often alluded to directly in mission statements and codes of ethics. If, as is frequently the case (and ought to be so), the business claims to value its people, do its recruitment processes, for example, live up to this? Are there clear job descriptions, objective selection criteria, etc. Is training and development really geared to allowing employees to do their jobs better and gain satisfaction and reward from their performance? Are there satisfactory grievance, disputes and appeals procedures?

Such questions and many others will try to elicit the extent to which justice and decency, the basic business values, are enshrined in the structures and processes of the organisation. Only thus will it become clear whether the claims of the mission statement and ethical codes are more than pious hopes. The relevance of all this for business activity is clear when it is remembered that a purely formal code which is unconnected to actual practice, or is contradicted by it, will not be merely neutral but directly damaging to the business's identity and its employee morale, customer faith and shareholder trust. The claim that 'we value our people' is better not made at all than accompanied by the lowest possible remuneration, inadequate or non-existent training or even poor food and insalubrious washrooms.

EXAMPLES OF ETHICAL AUDITS

It is worth looking at some frameworks, of greater or lesser complexity, which have been suggested and which relate specifically to ethics in organisations.

In their book *Good Business*, John Drummond and Sheena Carmichael suggest what they call 'the ethics test'.[13] This is partly a checklist for the individual and partly a company ethics checklist. Individuals are asked to say how they react to doing something they feel uncomfortable about (for example, do they lose sleep, drink too much, find they can't look people in the eye, try to find scapegoats?). They are then asked to say how they feel about business (that it's a jungle; that greed is good; that most business people are morally sound, etc.) and how they feel about their job (whether it satisfies them; makes them feel used; makes them proud of themselves and/or the company). Finally, individuals are asked whether they have ever done something they consider to be wrong at work, or felt under pressure to do so, or found a subordinate or superior has done something they consider to be wrong.

---

[13] S. Carmichael and J. Drummond, *Good Business: A Guide to Corporate Responsibility and Business Ethics*, Business Books, 1989, p. 81.

Having established an ethical awareness, Drummond and Carmichael go on to build up a Company Ethics Checklist which
provides some benchmarks against which a business can be
assessed. Such questions as whether the company is proud of its
products or services, comfortable and personal or anonymous
and impersonal, fair in promotions and remuneration, are
asked.[14] The checklist goes on to enquire whether the company
trusts its employees, has a rigid hierarchy, encourages aggressive-
ness or condones cut-throat competition. Finally, it asks whether
employees trust the company, trust the honesty of those at the
top and decisions made there, trust decisions made below and
feel that ethics is an explicit concern in the business.

All of this certainly raises ethical concerns and may focus
ethical awareness but it is not, as it stands, an ethical audit.
(Nor, it should be said in fairness, is this what the authors call
it; they have in mind more of a commonsense guide to ethical
issues in business.) It does not allow the business or its people
to assess with any accuracy the ethical commitment or success
of the business because it does not start from any clear statement
of the business's aim or values here. Rather, it takes some ethical
principles (being fair in promotions, trusting each other, being
honest and so on) and asks how, in a general way, individuals
think the company performs in relation to them. An audit, on
the other hand, needs to begin from an understanding of the
acknowledged purpose of the business, its values and standards,
before its ethical achievement can be judged.

At a rather more sophisticated level, Clutterbuck and Snow
sent questionnaires to some 800 companies which publicised
themselves as ethical organisations with an interest in social
responsibility programmes.[15] Based on the information they
received about company aims and practices in the areas of
ethics and responsibility, they constructed an audit framework which is a good deal more detailed than the general questions asked by Drummond and Carmichael. An audit attempts,
says Clutterbuck, 'to answer the management's need for infor-

---

[14] S. Carmichael and J. Drummond, *Good Business*, p. 87.
[15] Clutterbuck and Snow, *Working with the Community*, p.169. The response rate was
meagre; only 80 replied at all and only 42 sent back the whole questionnaire.

mation on where the organisation's performance is now, and where it ought to be'.[16] The audit will normally operate at *three* levels:

Policy

Are there documents which give the business's policy in the area?

Do people know that the policy exists and what it says?

Do the documents reflect the current state of knowledge and thinking?

Systems and standards

Do systems exist? Do they measure the right things?

Do they work? are they used?

Are standards high enough? Do they compare with best practice elsewhere?

Are standards clearly understandable? Can they be measured year on year?

Recording and analysing performance

current performance

as compared with previous year

as compared with targets set.

Systems and standards take time to set up and effort and commitment to maintain but, as Clutterbuck says, every area of business responsibility can be measured in this way. For example, customer service can be audited by questionnaire or focus group; complaints content and handling procedure can be analysed; repeat business monitored and so on. Supplier issues can be audited by attitude surveys, monitoring of the extent to which information is shared, etc. All such auditing too, should seek to assess the degree of involvement and commitment at the various levels in the organisation. If only top management is committed to continuous improvement in the company's performance here, the business aim is unlikely to be achieved.

Perhaps the most comprehensive ethical audit that has been undertaken in Britain is that done by the University of Central Lancashire in 1992. In an attempt to find out 'Do we practise what we preach?', the university instigated an investigation of its policies and practice and produced an Ethics and Values

---

[16] Clutterbuck and Snow, *Working with the Community*, p.181.

Audit report (EVA) which highlights both the strengths and weaknesses of this type of enquiry.[17] The report is not, as its foreword makes clear, merely 'a self-congratulatory essay' but tries to develop a methodology honestly to assess the extent to which the institution's statements of values are translated into actions.[18]

The auditors started largely from three documents, the university's mission statement, its Equal Opportunities Policy and its Charter for Management, all of which, the report says, 'focus firmly on people'.[19] They all talk in ethical terms about justice, fairness, lack of discrimination, integrity, openness and respect for other people. From interviews, questionnaires and other research methods, the researchers try to determine how far such values are put into practice and what can be done to improve ethical practice.

The results of the audit are less important than the methodology which emerges. The auditors found, as was to be expected, a somewhat mixed bag of results, where 'mutual respect and trust' rubbed shoulders with dissatisfaction with working conditions and 'supportive informal staff networks' were undermined by 'insignificant communication networks and poor information flow'.[20] A recurring theme of the audit report is the extent to which, in any organisation, there are at least two elements to ethical activity: the first is the policy statements it puts out (its codes and practices on values, equality, management practice, etc.); the second is the personal values and priorities of the employees at all levels in the organisation. The audit may be critical in identifying the areas of divergence between the two and in suggesting ways in which the formal codes may more clearly reflect the values of the organisation's people, or how the organisation's ethical policies may be more clearly explained to people.

The 'methodology' which this audit employs is, in reality, several research methods used in different ways, to elicit rather different perspectives. A long questionnaire, a series of semi-structured interviews, the completing of Value Identification Grids (allowing individuals to be ranked on a scale of values), along with case studies and policy and curriculum analysis, were

---

[17] C. Henry *et al.*, *EVA, Project Report of the Ethics and Values Audit*, University of Central Lancashire, 1992.
[18] Henry *et al.*, *EVA*, p. 3.
[19] Henry *et al.*, *EVA*, p. 1.
[20] Henry *et al.*, *EVA*, pp. 6–7.

all used. The result is, in the end, perhaps more confusing than merely eclectic and the fact that the researchers set up a telephone line to take comments and queries from staff, the results of which they themselves fed into the developing methodology, added another level of complexity to the process. This latter may not, it seems, merely be the use of an acceptably dialectical or iterative process but may involve an undue loss of research objectivity.

Yet it is perhaps mean-spirited to concentrate unduly on the methodological limitations (or excesses) of this brave and interesting experiment. Perhaps the greatest value of the EVA is that it shows that this kind of enterprise can indeed be undertaken. It may, at this stage, be imperfect but it is neither conceptually nor practically impossible. If it begins to move people from saying '*Why should* we do this kind of exercise?' to asking '*How can* we do it?', it will have been useful. What is needed to take the framework forward, however, is greater refinement of the structures within which it is conducted and a clearer connection between the identified values and the business practice.

POSTSCRIPTS TO AUDIT

Complaints

Customer or client complaints are sometimes seen as a waste of business time and as largely undeserved slurs on the organisation. They may therefore be treated in a dismissive or defensive way. Yet the business which develops a well-organised system for dealing quickly and effectively with complaints can both gain in public relations terms and also learn about its shortcomings in order to rectify them. Thus handled, complaints can be positive rather than negative; they give one index of the business's quality of service or product. Thus viewed, they are a kind of extension of the audit process and, like an audit, they must be taken account of and built on. To be successful in this role, a complaints procedure needs to be:

- impartial
- public
- accessible
- quick
- effective.

Unless it is impartial and its findings are made public, any complaints system will fail to ensure that justice is not only done but seen to be done. If it is not well publicised and accessible, it cannot be an instrument of redress for those who really need it. If it is slow or ineffective, it will simply compound the original perceived insult. If, on the other hand, the procedures are well ordered and a result is efficiently produced, the findings, whatever they may be, can be of positive benefit, not only to the complainant but also to the business.

Ombudsman

Value statements and codes of ethics are inevitably general statements of principle which it is often left up to employees themselves to interpret in specific situations. There may be codes of operating practices which relate to specific activities within a business (covering areas like supplier relations, policies on gifts or entertainment, etc.) but these again will have to be interpreted by individuals in specific situations. Where an individual employee is unhappy about conduct in the organisation, believing that this does not fulfil the standards required, it is important that there is a publicised process whereby concern can be aired and dealt with. The alternative, as has already been pointed out (in chapter 8), is to risk whistle-blowing outside the business, with all the risks of confusion, ill feeling and bad publicity this can bring.

The usual suggested course of action for employees who find themselves in this kind of situation is to report their concerns within the existing managerial structure, to an immediate superior or, if that superior is the subject of the uncertain behaviour, to the level above. It is, of course, important that publicity given to such a protocol should stress the confidential nature of such reports and underline that individuals will not be discriminated against for making them. (As with complaints, it is crucial to identify the positive value to the business of the reporting of any behaviour which is counter to the published standards of conduct.)

It may be worth while, as many American firms are now doing, to make sure there is a court of appeal. In serious cases of malpractice, employees may feel that behaviour is entrenched or condoned through several layers of management and that going even to their boss's boss is of no avail. There should therefore be the right to go to a designated person, high in the organisation, preferably reporting to the chairman, who will deal with concerns of this type. This ombudsman role may be under-taken by a single individual director, say, or by a number of people who are specifically charged with fulfilling this responsi-bility. Either way, the mechanisms exist, and are seen to exist, for taking seriously the ethical concerns of employees and for making sure, in cases of abuse, that, again, justice is not only done but seen to be done.

The whole thrust of the argument of this book has been that, in recognising and identifying explicit ethical frameworks, organisations can improve their own *business* practices and more easily achieve their *business* aim. The extent to which the formal systems are carried into practice, therefore, becomes crucial. There is no point in having an impeccable mission statement or unimpeachable codes of practice if these are not put into practice in the day-to-day activity of the business: indeed, the immaculate but irrelevant code can simply become an object of cynicism and derision, both inside and outside the business, thus undermining the achievement of its aim.

Audits are a way of bringing together the theory and the practice. They give a snapshot, at any one time, of how far the business has disseminated its ethical principles through the organisation. As such, they may be a crucial element in the iterative process which can aid the development of the ethical enterprise.

10

The shape of things to come

The '90s is the decade of corporate democracy.
(Professor John Pound)[1]

What impresses me about Japan is they have these statements about values and missions and they believe them. We
have them and nobody pays any attention.
(Professor Charles Handy)[2]

What should the ethical business look like? And why are we
now asking questions about the nature and ends of business, the
answers to which we seemed to take for granted in the past? It
has been the argument of this book that the aim of business is
to secure long-term owner value by selling its wares in as effective
and efficient a manner as it knows how. It is this aim, rather
than vague social concerns or existential preoccupations, which
differentiates business from other, perfectly acceptable but different, forms of social activity. The idea thus stated may seem
uncontentious, not to say obvious, but it is nevertheless not
universally accepted.

It is argued by some commentators – and assumed by many
more – that there is now much more to the game plan of modern
business than this basic, albeit intelligible end: that whatever
business may have been in the past, it is now a much more
complex social phenomenon with consequent social as well as
economic ends. The first part of this statement is clearly true:
business *is* more complex, more interrelated with other social

---

[1] Speaking on *The Money Programme*, BBC 2, 30 May 1993. Professor Pound's argument
was that showing a proper concern for corporate governance and other ethical issues
would make companies better investments and more popular with shareholders,
especially of the institutional variety.

[2] C. Handy, What is a company for?, *RSA Journal*, vol. 139, no. 5416, March 1991,
p. 241.

phenomena than before. It is also international and operates in a world of complicated economic and social interdependencies. But this does not mean that its *aim* has changed, although clearly, how it achieves that aim must take account of the changed framework within which it operates. Business may often, then, have a social role to play, not because it has become part of its *aim* to develop the inner cities or support the performing arts, but because these activities may be part of the means in the modern world, just as much as cutting costs or increasing margins, of achieving the proper *commercial* aim. It is, as I have said before, important to get things the right way round.

But some people go even further and argue not merely for a social but for an 'existential' aim for business, where work is seen as the main focus of personal development, and organisations as the vehicles of that development. Thus: 'Humans have the unique capacity . . . to envisage and create new communities regulated . . . by the goal of preserving and promoting our common humanity.'[3] Yet business is not fundamentally about 'promoting our common humanity'; it is about being a good bank or retailer or pharmaceutical company. The aims of business are not somehow rendered more profound or acceptable by attaching to them a spurious social or philosophical dimension. All this does is muddy the waters and stop us from concentrating on the real issue of business ethics – which is how to ensure right action in business. This latter is a difficult, fragmented, pragmatic process, as we have seen in trying to work out just how ethical principles can be put into practice. And it is helped not at all by assuming that ethical honour is somehow satisfied by presenting business as 'preserving and promoting our common humanity'.

To argue against this view of the nature and ends of business is not, of course, to deny either the truth of the observation that business is more complex than in the past, or that a business which neglects its stakeholders in the apparent pursuit of its commercial aim, is likely to fail despite its efforts in other areas. Rather, it is to attempt to see the nature of business with greater clarity. Instead of *adding in* all the factors which make for the

---

[3] J. Wilcox and S. Ebbs, The leadership compass, quoted in C. Henry *et al.*, *EVA Project Report of the Ethics and Values Audit*, University of Central Lancashire, 1992, p. 122.

possible achievement of the end as part of the end itself, it surely makes sense to start by *paring down* to the aim of the activity – and then to go on to identify the ways undoubtedly complex, in which that aim can be achieved. It is worth bearing this argument in mind as we go on to look at some of the discussions currently in progress on the nature and shape of modern business. This is an agenda which includes questions about how business should be organised; how it should perceive itself, its mission, its place in the world.

Such issues, in one form or another, are being addressed by business schools, captains of industry, public enquiries and government commissions: in the UK, first of all by the Cadbury Committee, then by various city bodies of accountants, actuaries and regulators all offering their ideas on the shape of businesses to come. The Royal Society for the Encouragement of Arts, Manufacture and Commerce (RSA), too, launched an enquiry into what 'tomorrow's company' should look like.

WHY ARE PEOPLE RETHINKING BUSINESS NOW?

It is not by chance that these issues are the recurring ones on the business agenda at this time. To begin with, Britain is having to cope with both European and international pressures which encourage a certain introspection. The European Union (EU) is busily trying to harmonise not only the legal frameworks within which business must operate but also the regulatory basis of commercial dealings. Business people are aware of the need, in this context, to think through issues of corporate governance, company structure as well as commercial aims and aspirations. And to compound this scenario, the collapse of the old Soviet Union has changed for ever the perception of capitalism and its place in the world. On the one hand, capitalism now seems established as not simply one of at least two possible ways of understanding the world, but as the only respectable economic framework. On the other hand, now that the 'Evil Empire' of communism has fallen, what establishes the legitimacy of the system which consistently opposed it?[4] When the USSR could

---

[4] 'The Evil Empire' was Ronald Reagan's phrase for the Soviet Union at the time when he was advocating the 'Star Wars' project. It was the last time a Western leader took

be identified as 'the enemy', it was relatively easy to take for granted the positive contribution of capitalist business not only to prosperity but to freedom and democracy. With the demise of 'the enemy' this is more difficult to do. Capitalism, in other words, was very much defined in terms of its opposite and now one side of the house of cards has fallen new definitions are essential if the other side is to be firmly based.

It is true, too, that business now, like so much social interchange, is international. Not only 'big business', as in the past, but quite small concerns are able, because of communications and global marketing, to sell their wares in foreign markets and are increasingly aware that they need to do so. There then arise all the problems of international stakeholder pressures which, if they have not been thought through in terms of the aims and objectives of business, may prove inimical to success.

Again, the very scope and influence of modern business makes it important to have an up-to-date view of its philosophy and structures. In 1989, for example, only nineteen countries in the world had a GDP larger than the revenue of General Motors.[5] It is this kind of statistic which makes people view businesses as potentially the new imperialists and encourages them quite reasonably to ask what drives organisations with such power. What are their aims and aspirations?

SOME THEORIES OF TOMORROW'S BUSINESS

In his Michael Shanks Memorial Lecture, Professor Charles Handy gave his account of what a business should be for.[6] He draws on his own experience in business to suggest that it is not really about profits but about human relationships. Having failed to anticipate the market for petrol in an isolated little town in Borneo, where he was local manager for an oil company, he suggests that the last thing in his mind when the petrol did finally arrive was 'the possibility of milking my monopoly position

such a full-blown anti-Communist position based on a clear moral denunciation of the Soviet system.

[5] Quoted in Mark Goyder, *Rethinking the Company*, RSA Occasional Paper, June 1992, p. 3.

[6] Handy, What is a company for?, pp. 231–41.

and trebling the price . . .' In fact, he goes on, 'I sold it at a
50 per cent discount to say I was sorry.' [7] His message is clear: his
concern for his customers was far greater than his consideration of
profits. Later, he suggests that it was not, in fact, his customers,
but 'if I'm honest, it was my own self-respect which drove
me and the need to preserve my reputation'.[8] Whatever the
psychological bases, however, the argument is that the aim of
the business should be to serve people and not to assure shareholder value.

Many recent theories of what business should be are, like
Professor Handy's, emphatic that profits are not what it is about.
The Bishop of Oxford, for example, writing on the morality of
business, also rejects the centrality of owner value. 'The business
of business is serving society', he says. Having said this, however,
all such arguments go on sooner or later to involve caveats of
the form that 'profits are not, of course, irrelevant'.[9] Professor
Handy also states, on the page after the incident described, 'Let
us be clear, profits – and good profits – are always essential.'
Always? Or just not in Borneo? The force of this kind of argument
is clear, however. Whether it puts people in general or society
or employees or the environment at the centre of business calcu-
lation, it denies the ultimate significance of profits – short-term
or longer term – as giving the apparently erroneous impression
that business is a commercial rather than a primarily social
activity.

It would be easy to say that there is simply no disjunction
here between the social and commercial aims, between stakeholder value and social values, and that both can be seen as a
part of business activity. Of course, business *is* a social activity,
in that it takes place in society. But so are politics, education,
medicine and the Arts. It does nothing to help differentiate
business, to specify its intrinsic character, to say that it is 'social'.
Similarly, business is a moral activity in that it involves relationships between individual human beings, which is the basis of all
moral action. However, this is not the same as saying that
business exists or ought to exist in order to make people better

[7] Handy, What is a company for?, p. 233.
[8] Handy, What is a company for?, p. 235.
[9] Rt. Revd. Richard Harries, Bishop of Oxford, The morality of good business, *Business Strategy Review*, vol. 4, issue 1, Spring 1993, p. 88.

moral agents. Once again, it is important to get things the right way round. The aim of business, which differentiates it from that of medicine (to cure people) or of the Arts (to edify or entertain), is to secure longer term owner value. It has been the argument of much of this book that there may be the closest possible relationship between the achievement of that aim, the consideration of many stakeholders and the pursuit of certain kinds of ethical action, but the aim remains, conceptually at least, separate from the methods of achieving it.

The RSA enquiry into *Tomorrow's Company* suggests a rather different and interesting approach. Mark Goyder, introducing the enquiry, asked some intriguing questions about the aim and purpose of business. Is it possible, he wanted to know, to recognise all the stakeholders in your aim while keeping that aim simple? Business leaders recognise that they have to balance the claims of many stakeholders but, equally, they approve the simplicity of the scoring system where profits, earnings per share and share price are very clear tests of business success. 'The great advantage of the Anglo-Saxon habit of concentrating upon shareholders at the expense of the other stakeholders is that people throughout the organisation have a measure for exactly what success is.'[10] And since he sees this measure as limited, he goes on to ask what additional measures of success we need.

Lying behind this question, of course, is the assumption that the aim of business is not simply to secure shareholder value in the long run, but to do this *while also* delivering value to customers, employees, the community and all the other stakeholders who have an interest in a particular business. But again, pleasing customers, attending to employees and securing community support are *not* the aim of business; they are not even *a part* of the aim. Rather they are means of attaining the aim. The measure of success which concentrates on shareholder value, therefore, is not mistaken, old-fashioned or one-dimensional but merely proper. Other measures (such, it is suggested, as training, new business development, community spending or environmental protection) are not, properly understood, aims or purposes at all but, again, ways of delivering the aim.

Some commentators, however, are not arguing merely for the

[10] Goyder, *Rethinking the Company* p. 5.

broadening of the business aim but for an entire upending of the 'financial culture' of British (and indeed Anglo-Saxon) business. Gottfried Bruder, general manager of the German Commerzbank in the UK, has argued, for example, that the very excellence of the UK's financial culture and the emphasis on shareholder value is actually undermining of industry and commerce.[11] The dominance of this culture, he suggests, inhibits investment in R&D, education and training and, significantly, in British companies the finance director is the most important executive after the chairman – and sometimes ahead of him. This diminishes the roles of all other players in the business, whether product planning, research, personnel or marketing: all are smothered by accountants and bankers.

The suggestion here is that aiming to make a profit may actually be undermining of that aim: that trying to secure long-term owner value may by that very act deny the possibility of achieving it. But, clever as the paradox thus presented is, it is surely only the case if the aim of business is once again confused with the methods of achieving that aim. The aim is indeed a commercial or, if you like, financial one, but the methods of achieving it are wider and more complex. In order to boost share price or enhance earnings per share, the business will have to take account of training, R&D, marketing and the rest and it is sheer sophistry to suggest that financial *aims* somehow confine the business to financial *means*.

WHAT SHOULD MODERN BUSINESS BE LIKE?

The ethical modern business, then, is not to be defined in terms of some nebulous social aim, but in terms of its proper business aim, and the essence of achieving this is in the long-term perspective and strategic vision which the successful business must adopt. Short-termist attitudes are often the most undermining of both ethical and commercial success. For example, in the late 1980s, mergers and acquisitions (M&A) flourished, partly as a result of the financial markets' willingness to lend. Companies ran the risk of being the target of what often became hostile takeover

---

[11] Gottfried Bruder, The systematic antagonisms within the British business culture, paper given at an Engineering Sector Dialogue Seminar, London, November 1992.

bids. There is nothing unacceptable or unethical in the nature of M&A and even hostile bids may have their place if their aim is to transform inefficient companies into successful ones. But the attitude which sees takeovers as a way of making short-term gains by simply breaking up and selling off can be inimical to both ethical standards and business practice. As one commentator says, 'The economy only works well if companies evolve over time, constantly improve efficiency and enhance the quality of their products in order to serve their customers to the best possible degree.'[12]

A short-term perspective means, too, that the interests of stakeholders, not only employees and customers but also shareholders, will be denied. If investment is forgotten, research and development ignored and training put off, long-term profitability is inevitably undermined. The immediate outcome will be an unethical relationship with employees and customers, who will not be nurtured as they would have to be in a business with a longer-term perspective, where their interests would be recognised as central to the achievement of success. In the slightly longer term, the business itself will cease to have a future.

The modern ethical enterprise will thus have a long-term view. Even if it cannot hope for eternal life, it will constantly have its eyes set on the future and on how it must change to secure that future. It will also be constantly aware of the systems and structures by which it operates. Achieving an ethical climate and ensuring right action in business relies on individuals doing the right thing but this cannot be taken to mean that individual attitudes are the main factor here. The ethical attitude and personal integrity of the top people is an essential component in establishing what the values and standards of the enterprise are. Employees look to the top to get a sense of 'what goes' in the organisation. But beyond this, business ethics are systemic rather than purely individual. This is not the view of all business people. For example, Ellen Schneider-Lenne, in her Stockton Lecture at the London Business School, ends by claiming that 'Good business is not so much about good systems as about good people.'[13]

[12] Ellen Schneider-Lenne, The governance of good business, *Business Strategy Review*, vol. 4, no. 1, Spring 1993, p. 78.
[13] Schneider-Lenne, Governance of good business, p. 85.

Although such a pronouncement is useful in redressing the balance away from the depersonalisation of ethics and focusing on individual responsibility, it rather obscures the way in which the organisation affects and influences individual action. 'Corporations are social cultures with character – character that can exercise good or bad influences, depending on goals, policies, structures, strategies and other characteristics that formalise relations among the individuals who make up corporations.'[14] So says Michael Hoffman, emphasising the importance of codes of ethics. He goes on, 'Causes of unethical actions are quite often systemic and not simply the result of rotten apples in the corporate barrel. Ethical people can be brought down by serving in a bad organisation, just as people with questionable ethical integrity can be uplifted or at least held in check by serving in a good one.'[15]

The importance of codes of corporate ethics and specific codes of practice (on anything from recruitment procedures to receipt of gifts and business entertaining) should not be underestimated. There is a tendency in looking at business ethics to lose sight of the basic aim, which can never be repeated too often. It is not to make people better moral agents, although this may be a welcome outcome of clearer ethical priorities, but to ensure right action in business. The claim that, fundamentally, what is required is a 'change in attitudes', that individuals have to be personally morally responsible for all their actions at work, should be resisted, not because individual moral responsibility is a bad thing but because the aim of achieving right action in business is not best served by relying purely on personal standards. 'Changing attitudes' is, in any case, notoriously a long-run strategy, and, as Keynes said, in the long run, we're all dead.

We need to influence *actions* now. Attitudes are less crucial than actions; the inner workings of consciences and beliefs are not really the main issue. When behaviour is changed, even if this is done by threat of sanctions, opinions and attitudes will often be modified to take account of this. Attitudes are not, of course, irrelevant: they reinforce and secure behaviour but they

[14] M. Hoffman, Developing the ethical corporation, in M. Hoffman and J. Moore, *Business Ethics: Readings and Cases in Corporate Morality*, McGraw-Hill, 1990, p. 629.
[15] Hoffman, Developing the ethical corporation, p. 630.

may not themselves be the critical variable. Which is perhaps just as well because, whereas we cannot achieve immediate changes in belief – in what people may feel deep down – we can, fairly dramatically and quickly, change behaviour. This is done largely by attention to the structures and systems of the business, which are critical in encouraging some types of behaviour and discouraging others. In short, we must ensure that the structures within which people operate make doing the *right* thing the *easiest* thing to do.

To rely on personal moral scrupulousness to ensure ethical action in business is both time-consuming and uncertain. It leaves people again on their own to apply their individual codes to the detail of corporate action. This is neither fair nor reliable. To have the right structures in place, then, is essential if the ethical organisation is to be achieved. This will probably involve both a code of conduct which identifies for *this business* the operational values and standards of conduct, and also a series of protocols which address particular areas or activities within the business and how they are to be carried out. The ethical code is important in identifying the business's aims, direction and values. Although it cannot, on its own, guarantee the achievement of the business aim, it has a number of specific business advantages:

It releases people *inside* the business from uncertainty about how they are expected to act and react; they do not have to spend time second-guessing a system which may seem to be telling them 'Do it – we don't care how.' And people who know they will be treated with justice and fairness can get on with the job rather than having to protect their own backs.

It allows people *outside* the business to identify positively what the business is offering and what they can expect when dealing with it. It offers transparency in crucial aspects of the business's arrangements, which is almost as important symbolically as it is substantively.

It *builds experience* and an idea of good practice in relations with all the stakeholders of the business and gets rid of the need for unsatisfactory, *ad hoc* responses to complex social and ethical issues.

In all these ways a code of ethics can help to ensure right action in business. This will probably need to be backed up too by protocols dealing with specific practices which spell out the business's values in a particular context. In recruitment, for example, it may be necessary to identify the processes by which equal opportunity is ensured. Unless objective criteria are applied, it is likely that the personal views and prejudices of the recruiters will come to the fore.[16] Informal channels of recruitment, informal selection criteria, informal interview processes, can all contribute to the overlooking or rejection of, say, women or ethnic minority candidates. In the same way, a protocol on promotion criteria may be needed to point up the relevance or otherwise of certain 'requirements' of the job. Is the need to be geographically mobile, for example, really a requirement of the job, or simply a rather crude measure of apparent commitment and ambition? It may be an impossible demand of, for example, an otherwise qualified woman with family commitments, becoming, in effect, a form of indirect discrimination.[17]

Ethical codes and protocols of business practice are not, therefore, simply banal claims to be on the side of the angels, without practical application or value. Rather, they can be essential tools in the pursuit of right action. Ethical organisations are less the product of changing attitudes in order to produce communities of saints than of the setting up of structures which encourage the not-so-bad to do the good – by making the right thing the easy thing to do.

AN INTERNATIONAL BUSINESS ETHIC?

Business is set to become more and more international. What relevance has business ethics in this marketplace where stakeholders have not only different social, cultural and economic viewpoints but perhaps different ethical priorities and perspectives? Can there be an international business ethic? Is any sensible dialogue possible between those of widely different cultures and value systems?

There is certainly more scope for an international code of

---

[16] This is graphically illustrated in relation to women applicants in D. Collinson *et al.*, *Managing to Discriminate*, Routledge, 1990.

[17] For a discussion of the practicalities of ensuring equal opportunities for women in employment, see E. Vallance, Women at work: a problem for business ethics, *Business Ethics: A European Review*, vol. 2, no. 1, 1993, p. 5.

business ethics than is generally assumed. It is normally believed that the diversity of actual circumstances invalidates any attempt to find universal principles of business practice. But the argument of this book has been that business can be designated by its aim – the production of owner value in the longer term. This is a universal definition whether the business is in Birmingham or Bombay. In addition, the key principles of business ethics are justice and common decency. The former asserts that, growing out of the nature and aim of business itself, rewards should be commensurate with contribution to the enterprise; the latter that, without the decent treatment of stakeholders, again, the very purpose of the business is likely to be undermined.

These principles are not the expressions of mere preference or personal taste or religious or cultural choice. If they were, it would be arrogant to suggest that they be universalised. Rather, they are based in the nature of business and the nature of ethics. Ethics is about universal principles of good and bad. Lying, cheating and stealing are simply wrong as are breaking of contracts or of promises. Justice and honesty are always right, be it in business or in any other social intercourse, in the UK or the Ukraine. Business ethics applies these general moral principles in the specifically business context in an attempt to clarify moral dilemmas in this area.

Of course, although it may be reasonably simple to identify ethical principles, it is not always easy to apply them. Justice and honesty may be clearly recognised as values but what is to *count* as honest or just may be contestable, especially if the two seem to be in conflict. However, we need to bear in mind that, in seeking to secure long-term owner value, a business cannot ignore the interests of any of its stakeholders: their preferences, including their moral preferences, will crucially influence their dealings with the business and will therefore have an effect on owner value. Given the different views of stakeholders in different parts of the world, it is hardly surprising that businesses vary as they do. Yet all are businesses and, operating within a market framework, presuming legal compliance, the system of business ethics based on the aim of the business is universally applicable, regardless of time and place, geography and culture.

How does this work out in practice? If we can apply universal ethical principles in business, does this mean we are stuck with

a framework which can take no account of what may be appropriate in differing situations, where we must act in the same way
regardless of times and places? Not necessarily: local conditions
will always be part of the equation. In the case of selling 'mature'
products or out-of-date equipment abroad, for example, ethical
principles do not necessarily dictate that no such transactions
are ever acceptable. To sell old-style record players to developing
countries where CD players are neither desired nor affordable
may be more a matter of market knowledge than imperialistic
condescension! The level of detail on food labelling may be
legitimately different in Somalia and Scotland; but one might
draw the line, even in a situation of famine, where sell-by dates
were systematically ignored. If a product is actually dangerous,
its sale would be wrong in any circumstances, and, in any case,
would be more likely to attract prosecution than repeat business.

The argument that it is possible to have an international
business ethic does not in any way deny the difficulty of making
moral decisions in transnational businesses: moral dilemmas,
choices between greys rather than between black and white will
always be there and be hard. However, when the nature and
aim of business and the principles of justice and decency which
have been developed in this book are borne in mind, it is often
possible to see ways through the ethical issues which arise in
the course of international transactions, and so to recognise
that these need be no more *ad hoc* than their local or national
equivalents.

ETHICS AS STRATEGY

As has been pointed out many times in the course of this book,
there is no *logical* connection between being ethical and being
successful in business. The good may founder and the bad may
prosper – at least for a time. Yet, as business ethics becomes
more and more talked about and 'high ethics' businesses are
more and more the exemplary cultures, it will become less and
less possible for businesses to ignore the ethical dimension of
their activity or to seek to marginalise it as the quirky concern
of a few big firms which can 'afford it'. As employees become
aware of their power as stakeholders in the business, as customers
demand to be taken note of, so shareholders too will increasingly

put their money where the ethics is. To do otherwise will seem like too high a risk.

There is increasing evidence too, the most recent from some research at Cornell University, that people not only prefer honesty to chicanery, but are surprisingly good at telling the decent and the cheats apart.[18] Narrowly self-interested behaviour, it seems, is ultimately self-defeating and ethics may thus become a strategic imperative rather than being seen, quite erroneously, as a merely abstract and ivory-tower concern.

It seems clear, in any case, that spelling out what you aspire to be, what your values and standards are, is becoming very important to modern businesses. People need, as never before, to see themselves regarded as part of the process of decision-making; they want to 'own' the business, not necessarily financially but, more importantly for them, in strategic and developmental terms. This does not mean there is no role for leadership; it is not possible to identify and drive through company values without vision and leadership. But leadership here needs to mean top-led, rather than top-down. As Max DePree has said, 'Leadership is a serious meddling in other people's lives, no matter how it is done.'[19] It can only be morally justified when it is itself informed by some ethical purpose and when it galvanises ideas and ideals into a vision for the enterprise as a whole.

The ethical enterprise of the future will need leadership of this top-led variety; it will also need vision. Much has been written about 'visionary' businesses and their need for charismatic leaders, but the most recent work in this area by the Stanford Business School professor James Collins suggests that both 'vision' and 'leadership' are much misunderstood terms. Charisma's place in setting vision, he says, is vastly overrated, and attempting to substitute charisma for substance – for real structures and systems – is destructive. He goes on, 'The function of a leader – the one universal requirement of effective leadership – is to catalyze a clear and shared vision of the organisation and to secure commitment to and vigorous pursuit of that vision . . . The key is to build an *organisation* with vision, not simply to

---

[18] Reported in *The Economist*, 29 May 1993, p. 85.
[19] M. DePree, The leadership quest: three things necessary, *Business Strategy Review*, vol. 4, no. 1, 1993, p. 69.

have a single charismatic *individual* with vision' (my emphases).[20] And ethical commitment can be a central part of the business vision; again, not merely as an inspirational ideal but as a part of business strategy. It is good *action* that is required, not simply pious hopes and good intentions. Visions can be counter-productive if they are merely talked about and never oper-ationalised; once again, it is the *structures* in terms of which the principles are put into practice which become critical here.

Structures, of course, can be overplayed. On their own, unin-formed by any vision of what they are there to achieve, they are flat and limited. Without an ethical ideal, business is two-dimensional: it may be financially and organisationally impec-cable but it only acquires real momentum when it recognises its aim and so acquires its ethical centre. Ethics is business's third dimension.

Ethics can also be business's strategic centre. Working out ethical problems, coping with ethical dilemmas, forces a business to think through its aims and aspirations and to relate these to its structures and strategy. The business's relations with all its stakeholders, too, can have enormous implications for its strategic direction. An overt ethical position may also give a business a direct competitive edge. Business ethics is not something which exists in a separate compartment from business itself, as a rarefied and therefore dispensable additional extra. To emphasise its strategic role in business is neither itself unethical nor overly instrumental. It is to identify the quite realistic, practical and central role that ethics plays in business practice. And if such a view robs ethics of some of its mystique by bringing it out of the clouds and down to the level of everyday decision-making, this is all to the good, for that is exactly where it ought to be.

---

[20] J. Collins and J. Porras, Organisational vision and visionary organisations, *California Management Review*, vol. 34, no. 1, 1991, p. 51.

Bibliography

There is a wide variety of introductory books in the area dealing both with the philosophical and conceptual problems of business ethics and with the practical implications of the social responsibility of business. I have chosen the ones which seem to me to be the clearest and most accessible and which, between them, cover more or less all aspects of the subject. The books are listed in alphabetical order. In some cases the titles are self-explanatory.

Until recently, the main journals were American and therefore focused on experience in the USA. The publication of *Business Ethics: A European Review* brought the European experience to the fore and is therefore of particular interest to British students of the subject.

Richard Adams, Jane Carruthers and Sean Hamil, *Changing Corporate Values*, Kogan Page, 1990. (A review of the values of top British businesses and a discussion of some of the issues surrounding these values.)

T. Beauchamp and N. Bowie, *Ethical Theory and Business*, 3rd edition, Prentice Hall, 1988. (Still one of the best introductory texts available, identifying and explaining the major issues.)

Sir Adrian Cadbury, *The Company Chairman*, Fitzwilliam Publishing, 1990. (The main issues of corporate governance looked at from the point of view of the chairman of the board.)

Tom Cannon, *Corporate Responsibility*, Pitman Publishing, 1992. (A very readable account of corporate social responsibility seen in relation to current social, political and economic forces.)

S. Carmichael and J. Drummond, *Good Business: A Guide to Corporate Responsibility and Business Ethics*, Century Hutchinson, 1989. (A guide to the application of ethics in business.)

D. Clutterbuck and D. Snow, *Working with the Community*, Weidenfeld and Nicolson, 1990. (A practical guide to social responsibility.)

John Donaldson, *Business Ethics, A European Casebook*, Academic press, 1992. (A case study approach to issues in business ethics.

Also includes the full text of the European Social Chapter and a discussion of the uses and limitations of ethical codes in business.)

Thomas Donaldson, *The Ethics of International Business*, Oxford University Press, 1992. (Outlines the particular ethical difficulties faced by multi-nationals.)

Gerard Elfstrom, *Moral Issues and Multi-national Corporations*, Macmillan, 1991. (Argues for a Utilitarian moral framework as the basis of ethical decision-making by multi-nationals.)

T. Foster, *101 Great Mission Statements: How the World's Leading Companies Run their Businesses*, Kogan Page, 1993.

M. Friedman, *Capitalism and Freedom*, University of Chicago Press, 2nd edition, 1982. (The classic statement of aims of capitalist business.)

Richard de George, *Business Ethics*, Macmillan, 1986. (A seminal introduction to the subject by one of its American gurus.)

Richard de George, *Competing with Integrity in International Business*, Oxford University Press, 1993. (A leading thinker's most recent thoughts on the perennial ethical dilemmas of international business.)

Charles Handy, *The Empty Raincoat: Making Sense of the Future*, Hutchinson, 1994. (A brilliant attempt to put the largely lost ethical dimension back into business organisations and relationships.)

W. M. Hoffman and J. M. Moore, *Business Ethics: Readings and Cases in Corporate Morality*, 2nd edition, McGraw-Hill, 1990. (A useful series of introductory readings grouped around the functional areas of business.)

J. Mahoney, *Teaching Business Ethics in the UK, Europe and the USA*, Athlone, 1990.

J. Mahoney and E. Vallance (eds.), *Business Ethics in a New Europe*, Kluwer Academic Press, 1992. (A collection of essays covering both conceptual and practical aspects of the European experience.)

R. Monks and N. Minow, *Power and Responsibility*, HarperCollins, 1991. (Exploring the problem of how to create trust between managers and shareholders through an effective structure of accountability.)

L. Nash, *Good Intentions Aside, A Manager's Guide to Resolving Ethical Problems*, Harvard Business School Press, 1990. (Attempts to outline a framework which will allow managers to articulate and act on their own 'common sense standards of integrity'.)

Robert C. Solomon, *Ethics and Excellence, Cooperation and Integrity in Business*, Oxford University Press, 1993. (A scholarly but accessible interpretation of the Aristotelean relationship between the individual and the community and of the connection between personal integrity and corporate ethics.)

S. Webley, *Business Ethics and Company Codes*, Institute of Business Ethics, 1992.

The main journals in the area, available in university and college libraries are:

Business Ethics, A European Review.

The Journal of Business Ethics.

Business and Professional Ethics Journal.

Harvard Business Review.

The Economist has strong coverage of business ethics and environmental issues.

The Financial Times from time to time publishes a section reviewing business books.

Index